MW00901552

THE PATH

TO

PROSPERITY

THE PATH
TO
PROSPERITY

A BLUEPRINT FOR AMERICAN RENEWAL

FISCAL YEAR 2013 BUDGET RESOLUTION
House Budget Committee
Chairman Paul Ryan of Wisconsin
Prosperity.budget.house.gov

Copyright © 2012

Published in the United States by Pacific Publishing Studio.

www.PacPS.com

ISBN-13: 978-1479129638

ISBN-10: 1479129631

No part of this book may be reproduced in any form unless written permission is granted from the author or publisher. No electronic reproductions, information storage, or retrieval systems may be used or applied to any part of this book without written permission.

Special acknowledgement is made to the following:

Prosperity.Budget.House.Gov

Due to the variable conditions, materials, and individual skills, the publisher, author, editor, translator, transcriber, and/or designer disclaim any liability for loss or injury resulting from the use or interpretation of any information presented in this publication.

While every effort has been made in the preparation of this material to ensure the information is accurate, the publisher, author, editor, translator, and/or transcriber assume no responsibility for errors and/or omissions. No liability is assumed for damages resulting from the use of the information contained herein.

TABLE OF CONTENTS

STATEMENT OF CONSTITUTIONAL AND LEGAL AUTHORITY

Article I of the U.s. Constitution grants Congress the power to appropriate funds from the Treasury, pay the obligations of and raise revenue for the federal government, and publish statements and accounts of all financial transactions.

In addition, the Congressional Budget and Impoundment Act of 1974 requires Congress to write a budget each year representing its plan to carry out these transactions in the forthcoming fiscal years. While the President is required to propose his administration's budget requests for Congress's consideration, Congress alone is responsible for writing the laws that raise revenues, appropriate funds, and prioritize taxpayer dollars within an overall federal budget.

The budget resolution is the only legislative vehicle that views government comprehensively. It provides the framework for the consideration of other legislation. Ultimately, a budget is much more than series of numbers. It also serves as an expression of Congress's principles, vision, and philosophy of governing.

This budget, submitted to the U.S. House of Representatives for fiscal year 2013 and beyond, builds upon the budget that was written and passed by the House last year. Like last year's budget, it is offered on time, in accordance with the 1974 Budget Act, out of respect for the law and in order that the public be given a timely and transparent accounting of government's work.

Like last year's budget, it is committed to the timeless principles enshrined in the U.S. Constitution - liberty, limited government, and equality under the rule of law.

And like last year's budget, it seeks to guide the nation's policies by those principles, freeing it from the crushing burden of debt now threatening its future.

This budget is submitted, as prescribed by law, to clarify the challenges and the choices facing the American people, provide a blueprint for the orderly execution of Congress's constitutional duties, and describe a path forward that renews the promise of this exceptional nation.

A Contrast in Visions

	The President's Budget	*The Path to Prosperity*
Spending	Net $1.5 trillion increase relative to current policy	Cuts spending by $5 trillion relative to President's budget
Taxes	Imposes a $1.9 trillion tax increase; Adds new complexity and new hurdles for hardworking taxpayers, making it more difficult to expand opportunity	Prevents President's tax increases; Reforms broken tax code to make it simple, fair, and competitive; clears out special interest loopholes and lowers everybody's tax rates to promote growth
Defcits	Four straight trillion-dollar deficits; Breaks promise to cut deficit in half by end of first terms; Budget *never* balances	Brings deficits below 3 percent of GDP by 2015; Reduces deficits by over $3 trillion relative to President's budget; Puts budget on path to balance
Debt	Adds $11 trillion to the debt - increasing debt as a share of the economy - over the next decade; Imposes $200,000 debt burden per household; Debt skyrockets in the years ahead	Reduces debt as a share of the economy over the next decade; Charts a sustainable trajectory by reforming the drivers of the debt; Pays of the debt over time
Size of Government	Size of government never falls below 23 percent of the economy, making it more difficult to expand opportunity	Brings size of government to 20 percent of economy by 2015, allowing the private sector to grow and create jobs
National Security	Slashes defense spending by nearly $500 Billion; Threatens additional cuts by refusing to specify plan of action to address the sequester; Forces troops and military families to pay the price for Washington's refusal to address drivers of debt	Prioritizes national security by preventing deep, indiscriminate cuts to defense; Identifies strategy-driven savings, while funding defense at levels that keep America safe by providing $554 billion for the next fiscal year for national defense spending
Health Security	Doubles down on health care law, allowing government bureaucrats to interfere with patient care; Empowers an unaccountable board of 15 unelected bureaucrats to cut Medicare in ways that result in restricted access and denied care for current seniors, and a bankrupt future for the next generation	Repeals President's health care law; Advances bipartisan solutions that take and put patients in control; No disruption for those in or near retirement; Ensures a strengthened Medicare program for future generations, with less support given to the wealthy and more assistance for the poor and the sick

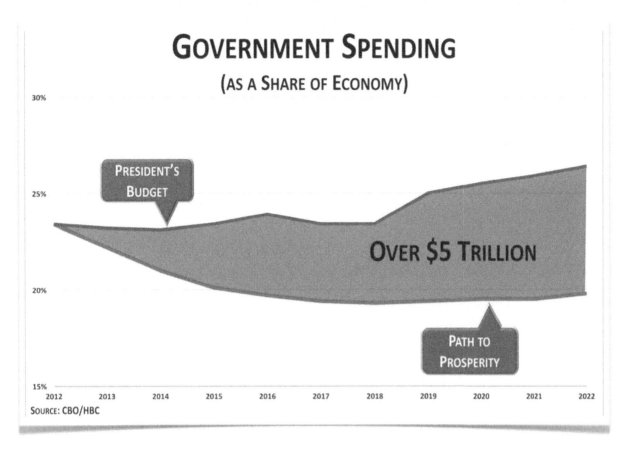

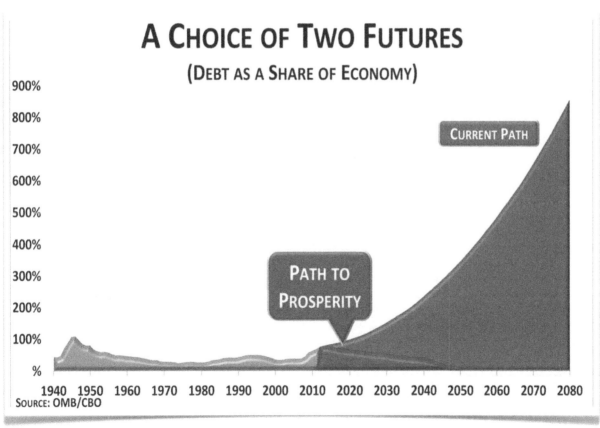

INTRODUCTION
By House Budget Committee Chairman Paul Ryan

This budget offers a blueprint for safeguarding America from the perils of debt, doubt and decline. Americans, not Washington, deserve to choose the path their nation takes, and this budget presents a clear choice between the bleak future toward which the nation is currently headed and the prosperous future that Americans can build together with a government that is limited and effective.

Effective government is impossible without limits. It is no surprise that trust in government has reached all-time lows as the size of government has reached all-time highs. The Founders put limits *on* government because they understood the limits *of* government. In James Madison's formulation, "If men were angels, no government would be necessary. And if angels were to govern men, neither external nor internal controls on government would be necessary.' As Madison reminded us, men are no angels, and government is "administered by men over men.'

The Founders met this challenge by designing a Constitution of enumerated powers, giving the federal government broad authority over only those matters that must have a single national response, while sharply restricting its authority to intrude on those spheres of activity better left to the states and the people.

The first responsibility of the federal government is the safety and security of all Americans. Today, the men and women of the U.S. military valiantly devote themselves to protecting American lives and liberty. Peace at home is only possible when America is strong. When America shrinks from her commitments to her allies and her duties to her citizens, her enemies are emboldened and her ideals are diminished. This overarching governmental responsibility - securing the inherent rights of all Americans to life, liberty, and the pursuit of happiness - is the principle and the purpose that informs this entire federal budget.

The federal government also has a critical role to play in safeguarding the free-enterprise system, so that fraud is punished, success is rewarded, and the rules are not rigged against the small businessman, the innovator, or the worker. In Abraham Lincoln's words, the true object of government should be "to clear the paths of laudable pursuit for all,' so that all may have the same opportunity to rise.

The federal government can help provide a strong safety net for Americans who, through no fault of their own, have fallen on hard times. But government can never replace the core institutions of a vibrant civil society - families, neighbors, churches and charities. Aimed first and foremost at buttressing these institutions, government reforms should promote upward mobility and secure opportunity, especially for society's most vulnerable.

Over the past century, the American people have sought to furnish a strong and stable base of health and retirement security for working families. In a free society built on entrepreneurial risk-taking and hard work, such protection provides insurance against the vagaries of life. But when government mismanagement and political cowardice turn this element of the social contract into an empty promise, seniors are threatened with denied access to care and the next generation is threatened with a debt that destroys its hard-earned prosperity.

Both consequences would violate President Lyndon B. Johnson's pledge upon signing the Medicare law: "No longer will older Americans be denied the healing miracle of modern medicine. No longer will young families see their own incomes, and their own hopes, eaten away simply because they are carrying out their deep moral obligations to their parents, and to their uncles, and to their aunts.' To fulfill Johnson's pledge in the 21st century, America's generations-old health and retirement security programs must be saved and strengthened.

5

The federal government has the power to raise revenue so that it can effectively carry out those missions entrusted to it by its citizens. But when taxation is carried to injurious excess to fund activities outside the proper sphere of government, it not only harms the general welfare, but also suppresses revenue itself. As Alexander Hamilton - whose fiscal plan brought national prosperity while eliminating America's first federal debt - once observed, "the most productive system of finance will always be the least burdensome.'

Finally, the federal government has an obligation to all Americans to account for the spending, taxing, and borrowing that it undertakes in their names. But when the federal budgeting process is ignored, government spends haphazardly, without priorities or the transparency on which democracy depends.

In each of these core areas, the unchecked growth of government has degraded its effectiveness and rendered its institutions incapable of meeting the challenges of the 21st Century.

- The U.s. military faces a three-fold threat: an abatement of America's commitment to defend its interests abroad, a slow economy, and an uncontrolled debt burden that weakens America from within by eroding resources for national defense;
- The free enterprise system is being stifled by a federal bureaucracy fixated on depriving citizens and businesses of their ability to make social and economic decisions according to what is best for their own needs and interests.
- The social safety net is failing society's most vulnerable citizens and poised to unravel in the event of a spending-driven debt crisis, which is precisely when Americans would need it most;
- The future of the nation's health and retirement security programs is increasingly based on empty promises from a government unwilling to advance solutions that save and strengthen them;
- The tax code has become a broken maze of complexity and political favoritism; it is overgrown with special-interest loopholes and characterized by high rates, both of which stifle economic growth and job creation; and
- The federal budget process has collapsed, allowing government to spend recklessly and throw tax dollars at problems on an *ad hoc* basis as the nation's fiscal hole grows deeper.

The good news is that solutions to these problems are more attainable today than they have been in years: There is an emerging consensus - led by citizens across the nation and reformers across the political spectrum - that is well aware of the danger. This consensus rejects politicians who focus on dividing Americans for political gain. Instead, it supports bold reforms that bring Americans together to build upon the solid foundations of security and liberty that have made this nation exceptional:

- A military that keeps America safe by letting national strategic priorities determine spending levels, not the other way around;
- A free enterprise system that is reinvigorated, with bureaucracy restrained, the rule of law restored, and cronyism and corporate welfare eliminated;
- A safety net that directs assistance to those who need it most, provides greater incentives to work and save, and strengthens programs aimed at job training and helping Americans get back on their feet;
- Health and retirement programs that avert the sharp disruptions to come as a result of the President's policies, protect key commitments to seniors, and provide greater choices, better health, and real security for future generations;
- A tax code that fosters growth and job creation by lowering rates and getting rid of special-interest loopholes that mainly benefit the politically well-connected, distort economic growth, and encode unfairness in tax law; and
- A budget process that restrains government spending and restores certainty by forcing policymakers to provide solutions for the nation's fiscal future.

This nation has faced many tests in its history - moments in time when the very idea of America was threatened by crises at home and abroad. Each time, Americans rejected radical proposals to remake this exceptional nation in the image of less-free nations abroad. Instead, principled leaders and brave citizens rose to meet the difficulties they faced by applying the nation's enduring founding principles to the challenges of their times.

Today, America is struggling to recover from a great recession. Her people's liberties are endangered by unwarranted expansions of government. And she is threatened by a rising tide of debt at home and fierce enemies abroad. But as the challenge grows, so does the opportunity to restore America's promise and prosperity. In the words of Winston Churchill, this generation has the opportunity "to rejoice in the responsibilities with which destiny has honored us. And be proud that we are guardians of our country in an age when her life is at stake." We must not let this opportunity slip away.

This budget serves as a blueprint for American renewal. Its principled reforms empower individuals with greater control over their futures. It places great faith in the wisdom of the Founders and promises to renew confidence in the superiority of human freedom. The choice of two futures presented in this budget is premised on the wisdom of the American people to build a prosperous future for themselves and for generations of Americans to come.

Paul Ryan Chairman of the House Budget Committee Member of Congress, First District of Wisconsin March 20, 2012

A Blueprint for American Renewal

A Nation Challenged

The challenges this nation faces are among the largest in its history.

For years, bad policies advanced by both political parties have contributed to an irresponsible build-up of debt in the economy, and this debt now poses a fundamental challenge to the American way of life.

This build-up of debt has manifested its effects in both the private and public sectors. In 2008, excessive leverage in the financial sector overwhelmed many banks, businesses and families. Irresponsible decisions in Washington and on Wall Street fueled a housing-price bubble that collapsed and turned mortgage-backed securities into "toxic assets.' It soon became clear that these assets, which were spread throughout the financial sector, posed a systemic risk to the economy. The resulting wave of panics, bankruptcies and foreclosures brought the global financial system to the brink of collapse.

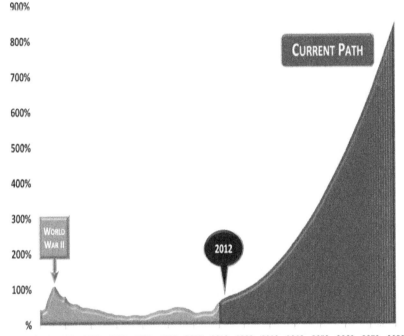

FIGURE 1

CRUSHING BURDEN OF DEBT
(U.S. DEBT HELD BY PUBLIC AS A SHARE OF ECONOMY)

SOURCE: OMB/CBO

America is still living with the painful consequences of that crisis today. While some of the federal government's emergency actions in late 2008 helped to stem the immediate financial crisis, much of its intervention in the wake of the crisis simply aggravated the underlying problems. In most cases, policymakers sought to address the symptoms of the crisis by transferring private-sector debt to the public balance sheet. Since Election Day 2008, debt held by the public has increased by roughly $4.5 trillion - an increase in excess of 70 percent in a mere four years.

This remedy didn't just ignore the underlying cause of the problem - it made the problem far worse. In Europe, the accumulation of public-sector debt now threatens to cause an even bigger calamity than the one caused by private-sector debt in 2008. The world's new "toxic asset' is the sovereign debt of irresponsible European governments, infecting the balance sheets of major banks and threatening the stability of the global economy. And in the United States, government debt continues to rise at a frightening pace, raising fears that a similar crisis may happen here.

The growing possibility of such a crisis is creating debilitating uncertainty about the future, hurting job creation and economic growth today. The economy has picked up in recent quarters, but overall growth and job creation remain subpar, and unprecedented numbers of Americans have simply given up trying to find work. Real GDP grew by just 1.7 percent in 2011, and private-sector forecasters are calling for growth of 2.3 percent in 2012 - well below the 3.0 percent historical trend rate of U.s. growth and just a fraction of the growth pace observed in a typical recovery from recession. Noted economists, including Federal Reserve Chairman Ben Bernanke, have argued that enacting a credible plan to deal with America's long-term debt build-up would have a positive effect on growth and jobs immediately.[1]

[1] For more detail, see "Debt as an Impediment to Growth' on page 74 of this report.

Unfortunately, in the years following the meltdown, the President and his party's leaders failed to use their full control of Washington to offer any plan to lift the debt and foster sustainable economic growth. Instead, the crisis was used as an excuse to enact unprecedented and counterproductive expansions of government power. A massive stimulus package failed to deliver promised reductions in unemployment. An unpopular health care takeover was jammed through Congress on a party-line vote. A short-sighted financial-regulatory overhaul failed to fix what was broken on Wall Street and made future bailouts more likely. And federal policymakers in thrall to a misguided form of environmental activism pushed through regulations and other policies that are making energy more expensive in the midst of a weak economy.

Through it all, the government's fiscal position sharply deteriorated. Total federal debt has now surpassed the size of the entire U.S. economy. And the government's non-partisan auditors have issued report after report warning of even larger debts to come, driven by health and retirement security programs that are being weakened by severe demographic and economic challenges.

Instead of taking action, the administration punted the nation's fiscal problems to a bipartisan commission, whose recommendations it proceeded to ignore in favor of proposals filled with gimmicks instead of real solutions. And the Democratic leaders of the senate have abandoned altogether their legal obligation to provide a budget plan - it has been three years since the senate passed a budget.

A Choice of Two Futures

Both parties share the blame for failing to take action over the years. But while Republicans offered a budget last year that would lift the crushing burden of debt and restore economic growth, the President and his party's leaders are still refusing to take seriously the urgent need to advance credible solutions to the looming fiscal crisis. Instead, they are still offering little more than false attacks and failed leadership.

Questioned about this disappointing reality at a recent House Budget Committee hearing, Treasury Secretary Timothy Geithner admitted, "We're not coming before you to say we have a definitive solution to our long-term problem. What we do know is we don't like yours."[2] The President's strategy seems to amount to this: Let somebody else propose a path forward, and then attack them for political gain.

This budget offers a better path. The following report lays out the challenge - and the choice - that America faces in each key area of the budget. The common thread connecting them all is that a sharp and sudden debt crisis would threaten the entire American project: It would weaken national security, shred the safety net that vulnerable Americans rely on, break promises to seniors, impose massive tax increases on families, and leave all Americans with a diminished future.

This looming crisis represents an enormous challenge, but it also represents a defining choice: whether to continue down the path of debt, doubt and decline, or put the nation back on the path to prosperity. It also represents a tremendous opportunity for this generation of Americans to rise to the challenge, as previous generations have, and fulfill this nation's unique legacy of leaving future generations with a freer, more prosperous America.

A Blueprint for American Renewal

This budget sets forth a model of government guided by the timeless principles of the American Idea: free enterprise and economic liberty; limited government and spending restraint; traditional family and community values; and a strong national defense.

The federal government has strayed from these American principles. This budget offers a set of fundamental reforms to put the nation back on the right track.

Timothy Geithner, Testimony before the U.S. House, Committee on the Budget, *The President's Fiscal Year 2013 Budget: Revenue and Economic Policy Proposals*, February 16, 2012.

House Budget Committee I March 20, 2012

The role of the federal government is both vital and limited. When government takes on too many tasks, it usually does not do any of them very well. Limited government also means effective government. This budget recommits the federal government to the security of every American citizen's natural right to life, liberty and the pursuit of happiness, while fostering an environment for economic growth and private-sector job creation.

1. Prioritize Defense Spending to Keep America Safe

With American men and women in uniform currently engaged with a fierce enemy and dealing with emerging threats around the world, this budget takes several steps to ensure that national security remains government's top priority.

Providing for the common defense: This budget rejects proposals to make thoughtless, across-the-board cuts in funding for national defense. Instead, it provides $554 billion for national defense spending, an amount that is consistent with America's military goals and strategies. This budget preserves necessary defense spending to protect vital national interests today and ensures future real growth in defense spending to modernize the armed forces for the challenges of tomorrow.

Reprioritizing sequester savings to protect the nation's security: The defense budget is slated to be cut by $55 billion, or 10 percent, in January of 2013 through the sequester mechanism enacted as part of the Budget Control Act of 2011. This reduction would be on top of the $487 billion in cuts over ten years proposed in President Obama's budget. This budget eliminates these additional cuts in the defense budget by replacing them with other spending reductions. Spending restraint is critical, and defense spending needs to be executed with effectiveness and accountability. But government should take care to ensure that spending is prioritized according to the nation's needs, not treated indiscriminately when it comes to making cuts. The nation has no higher priority than safeguarding the safety and liberty of its citizens from threats at home and abroad.

2. End Cronyism and Restore Free Enterprise

A growing economy, increased employment and higher wages will come from traditional American ingenuity and enterprise, not from government. To achieve this end, small businesses need to be empowered, and the size and scope of Washington need to be reduced so that the hard work and enterprise of Americans can lead a strong, sustained recovery.

Ending corporate welfare: There is a growing and pernicious trend of government overreach into the private economy -a trend that stacks the deck in favor of entrenched interests and stifles growth. This budget stops Washington from picking winners and losers across the economy. It rolls back corporate subsidies in the energy sector. It ends the taxpayer bailouts of failed financial institutions, including Fannie Mae and Freddie Mac. It repeals the government takeover of health care and begins to move toward patient-centered reform. And it reduces the bureaucracy's reach by applying private-sector realities to the federal government's civilian workforce.

Boosting American energy resources: Too great a percentage of America's vast natural resources remain locked behind bureaucratic barriers and red tape. This budget lifts moratoriums on safe, responsible energy exploration in the United States, ends Washington policies that drive up gas prices, and unlocks American energy production to help lower costs, create jobs and reduce dependence on foreign oil.

Streamlining other government agencies: Domestic government agencies have grown too much and too fast over the past decade, and much of their funding has gone to harmful programs and dead-end projects. This budget starts to restore spending discipline. It builds on efforts undertaken last year to contain the government's growth, and it targets hundreds of government programs that have outlived their usefulness.
' For more details, see Appendix II of this report.

3. Strengthen the Social Safety Net
This budget builds upon the historic progress of bipartisan welfare reform in the late 1990s. It strengthens Medicaid, food stamps and job-training programs by providing states with greater flexibility to help recipients build self-sufficient futures for themselves and their families.

Repairing a broken Medicaid system: Medicaid's flawed financing structure has created rapidly rising costs that are nearly impossible to check. Mandate upon mandate has been foisted upon states under the flawed premise that the best ideas for repairing this important health care safety net can come only from Washington. This budget ends that misguided approach and instead converts the federal share of Medicaid spending into a block grant, thus freeing states to tailor their Medicaid programs to the unique needs of their own populations.

Prioritizing assistance for those in need: The welfare reforms of the 1990s, despite their success, were never extended beyond cash welfare to other means-tested programs. This budget completes the successful work of transforming welfare by reforming other areas of America's safety net to ensure that welfare does not entrap able-bodied citizens into lives of complacency and dependency.

Ensuring educational and job-training opportunities for a 21st century economy: The government's well-intentioned approach to higher education and job training in America has failed those who most need these forms of assistance. Federal tuition subsidies are often captured by (and to a certain extent drive) rapidly rising tuition costs for those higher-education programs that should be the first rung on the ladder of opportunity. Meanwhile, dozens of job-training programs suffer from overlapping responsibilities and too often lack accountability.

This budget begins to address the problem of tuition inflation and consolidates a complex maze of dozens of job-training programs into more accessible, accountable career scholarships aimed at empowering American workers with the resources they need to pursue their dreams.

4. Fulfill the Mission of Health and Retirement Security

This budget puts an end to empty promises from Washington, offering instead real security through real reforms. The framework established in this budget ensures no disruptions to existing health and retirement benefit programs for those beneficiaries who have organized their retirements around them, while at the same time building stronger programs that future beneficiaries can count on when they retire.

Saving Medicare: Medicare is facing an unprecedented fiscal challenge. Its failed reliance on bureaucratic price controls, combined with rising health care costs, is jeopardizing seniors' access to critical care and threatening to bankrupt the system - and ultimately the nation. This budget saves Medicare by fixing flaws in its structure so it will be there for future generations. By putting these solutions in place now, this budget ensures that changes will not affect those in and near retirement in any way.

When younger workers become eligible for Medicare a decade or more from today, they will be able to choose from a list of guaranteed coverage options, including a traditional Medicare fee-for-service plan. This flexibility will allow seniors to enjoy the same kind of choices in their plans that members of Congress enjoy. Medicare will provide a payment to subsidize the cost of the plan, and forcing plans to compete against each other to serve the patient will help ensure guaranteed affordability. In addition, Medicare will provide increased assistance for lower-income beneficiaries and those with greater health risks. Reform that empowers individuals - with a strengthened safety net for the poor and the sick - will guarantee that Medicare can fulfill the promise of health security for America's seniors.

Advancing social security solutions: The risk to social security, driven by demographic changes, is nearer at hand than most acknowledge. This budget heads of a crisis by calling on the President *and* both chambers of Congress to ensure the solvency of this critical program.

5. Enact Pro-Growth Tax Reform

This budget recognizes that the nation's fiscal health requires a vibrant, growing private sector. It charts a prosperous path forward by reforming a tax code that is overly complex and unfair.

Individual tax reform: The current code for individuals is too complicated, with high marginal rates that discourage hard work and entrepreneurship. This budget embraces the widely acknowledged principles of pro-growth tax reform by proposing to consolidate tax brackets and lower tax rates, with just two rates of 10 and 25 percent, while clearing out the burdensome tangle of loopholes that distort economic activity.

Corporate tax reform: American businesses are overburdened by one of the highest corporate income tax rates in the developed world. The perverse incentives created by the corporate income tax do a lot of damage to both workers and investors, yet the tax itself raises relatively little revenue. This budget improves incentives for job creators to work, invest, and innovate in the United States by lowering the corporate rate from 35 percent to a much more competitive 25 percent and by shifting to a territorial system that will ensure a level playing field for American businesses.

6. Change Washington's Culture of Spending

Across the political spectrum, experts agree that the budget process is badly broken and in need of reform. The process fails to control spending, fails to provide adequate oversight, and fails to allow the transparency needed for accountability to the nation's citizens.

Controlling spending: The budget process in Washington contains numerous structural flaws that bias the federal government toward ever-higher levels of spending. This budget would lock in savings with enforceable spending caps and budget process reforms, limiting what Washington spends and how tax dollars are spent.

<u>Enhancing oversight:</u> This budget gives Congress greater tools to perform oversight over wasteful Washington spending.

<u>Increasing Transparency:</u> This budget promotes reforms that would give taxpayers more information over how Washington is spending their hard-earned dollars.

7. Lift the Crushing Burden of Debt

This budget charts a sustainable path forward, ultimately erases the budget deficit completely, and begins paying down the national debt.

Americans truly face a monumental choice - a choice that can no longer be avoided.

The Path to Prosperity advances the serious conversation begun last year about the future of this exceptional nation and the fundamental choices Americans must soon make about the kind of nation they want America to be.

This budget would put in place a comprehensive framework to address the nation's greatest challenges. It provides a blueprint for the actual work of statecraft. The elected representatives of the American people - in the House of Representatives, in the senate and in the White House - now must take up this budget and start building the future Americans deserve.

PROVIDING FOR THE COMMON DEFENSE

KEY POINTS

☑ The safety and security of the American people is the first responsibility of the federal government.

☑ The U.S. military is threatened by an uncontrolled debt burden that weakens America – but defense spending is not the driver of that debt burden.

☑ Despite this fact, the President's budget refuses to address runaway entitlement spending, and instead imposes nearly $500 billion in defense cuts over the next decade.

☑ This budget funds defense at levels that keep America safe by providing $554 billion for the next fiscal year - $6.2 trillion over the next decade - for national defense spending, an amount that is consistent with America's military goals and strategies.

☑ This budget replaces the indiscriminate reduction in defense spending scheduled to take place under the sequester with targeted reductions in non-defense mandatory spending. This protects defense from cuts that would jeopardize critical missions and the well-being of soldiers and their families.

☑ America's troops should not pay the price for Washington's failure to take action.

PROVIDING FOR THE COMMON DEFENSE

The Challenge: A Military Threatened

The first job of government is to secure the safety and liberty of its citizens from threats at home and abroad. Like all categories of government spending, defense spending should be executed with efficiency and accountability. However, because it is the first responsibility of government, the national defense should be funded based on *strategic*, not merely *budgetary*, calculations.

The United States spends a great deal on defense in nominal terms, but defense spending is shrinking as a share of government spending and as a share of the national economy. The share of the nation's resources devoted to defense has declined from its Cold War average of 7.5 percent to just 4.6 percent today. And defense spending constituted around 20 percent of federal spending in fiscal year 2011 - below the 25 percent it constituted just 30 years ago.

Defense's share of the budget is projected to shrink even further in the years ahead as other areas of the budget grow to unsupportable levels. This category of spending is clearly not driving the unsustainable fiscal trajectory that is threatening the nation's future.

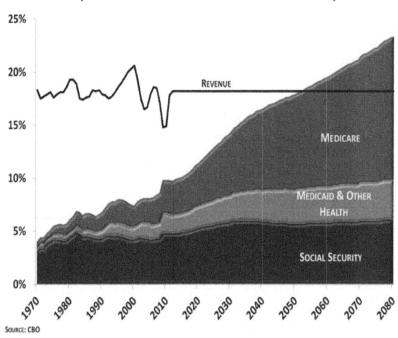

FIGURE 2

WHAT DRIVES OUR DEBT?
(GOVERNMENT SPENDING AS A SHARE OF ECONOMY)

SOURCE: CBO

Simply put, America's dangerous debt trajectory has put fiscal policy on a collision course with her national security, for two reasons.

First, Figure 2 makes it very clear that, absent action, social security, Medicare and Medicaid will soon grow to consume every dollar of revenue that the government raises in taxes. At that point, policymakers would be left with no good options. Making do without any federal government departments, including the military, is not really an option at all, and neither is raising taxes to a level that no free and prosperous economy could sustain.

Of course, if Congress continues to ignore the drivers of the debt, it will lose even the ability to make such choices on its own terms. The foreign governments and institutional lenders that finance America's debt would cut up the nation's credit cards before things got that far, representing a sudden and severe threat to the nation's ability to defend itself.

second, the Budget Control Act (BCA) signed into law last year created an automatic sequester process to force $1.2 trillion in spending reductions over ten years in the event that Congress failed to produce equivalent reductions through a specially formed Joint select Committee on Deficit Reduction (JsCDR). The BCA further specifies that, after accounting for reductions in debt-service costs, a total of $984 billion in net spending reductions is to be distributed equally among defense and non-defense accounts - resulting in a $492 billion reduction in each. To put this in perspective, defense constitutes approximately 20 percent of total federal spending, but will bear 50 percent of the spending reductions through sequestration.

Because the JsCDR failed to produce a bill, the sequester is scheduled to take effect beginning in January of 2013. While the sequester serves an important role in forcing Congress to reduce spending, it is vital that those spending reductions be done in a responsible way. Therefore, policymakers in both parties agree that the sequester should be replaced with equivalent deficit reduction to ensure that the national defense is not compromised.
A responsible budget must recognize that the United States is a nation with global interests, and that protecting those interests requires a strong, modern and capable military. The Constitution charges Congress with the responsibility for structuring, building, maintaining, and funding that military capability. It is a responsibility policymakers must make a top priority.

The Choice: Decline as a World Power vs. Renewed American Leadership

America's fiscal problems pose a real threat to its military, and left unaddressed, these problems will spell decline for America as a world power. The need to address this threat is urgent. But decline is not a certainty for America. Rather, as *Washington Post* syndicated columnist Charles Krauthammer put it, "decline is a choice."[4]

Letting budgetary concerns drive national-security strategy means choosing decline. By contrast, putting defense first among government's priorities while simultaneously lifting the debt burden and ensuring a more prosperous America would enable the nation to afford a modernized military that is properly sized for the breadth of the challenges America faces.

Decline as a World Power

On January 5, 2012, President Obama announced new defense strategic guidance premised on the hope that "the tide of war is receding."[5] But in testimony before the House Budget Committee, secretary of Defense Leon Panetta acknowledged that the administration's defense drawdown is being carried out in the face of ongoing elevated threats to the United states:

> SECRETARY PANETTA: But despite what we have been able to achieve, unlike past drawdowns when threats have receded, the United states still faces a complex array of security challenges across the globe: We are still a nation at war in Afghanistan; we still face threats from terrorism; there is dangerous proliferation of lethal weapons and materials; the behavior of Iran and North Korea threatens global stability; there is continuing turmoil and unrest in the Middle East; rising powers in Asia are testing international relationships; and there are growing concerns about cyber intrusions and attacks.[6]

Yet, the defining characteristic of the President's new defense posture is a reduction in the administration's own defense plan from last year, bringing the total reduction to $487 billion over the next ten years.

This number stands out as significant for several reasons. In the President's latest budget proposal, total spending increases by $1.5 trillion and taxes increase by $1.9 trillion, for a total of around $400 billion of deficit reduction over ten years. A clear-eyed look at the numbers reveals that American taxpayers and the Department of Defense are being asked to bear the entire burden of deficit reduction under the President's budget.

[4] Charles Krauthammer, "Decline is a Choice, *The Weekly Standard*, October 19, 2009.
http:iiwww.weeklystandard.comiContentiPubliciArticlesioooioooio17io56lfnpr.asp

[5] President Barack Obama, "Defense strategic Guidance Briefing,' January 5, 2012.
http:iiwww.defense.govitranscriptsitranscript.aspx?transcriptid=4953

[6] Leon E. Panetta, Testimony before the U.S. House, Committee on the Budget. *The Department of Defense and the Fiscal Year 2013 Budget*, February 29, 2013. http:ii budget.house.goviUploadedFilesiPanetta Testimony 2292012.pdf

Without the defense cuts, there would be no deficit reduction, and without the tax increases, the President's budget would represent $1.5 trillion in additional borrowing to finance new "stimulus' spending.[7] Under the President's budget, while all other government agencies enjoy a generous net increase in their allowance, only the federal government's highest priority - defense - is forced to make do with less.

The President has asserted that his new defense posture is driven by strategy and not budgets, but his timing indicates otherwise - he announced the budget figure at the same time he was announcing the beginning of his strategy review.

Rather than choosing to lead by addressing the fundamental drivers of near- and long-term deficits and debt, the President has defaulted to slashing the defense budget. The unmistakable fact is that the President has chosen to subordinate national-security strategy to his other spending priorities.

Renewed American Leadership

A robust national defense for generations to come can only be sustained on a sound economic foundation. A safer world and a more prosperous America go hand-in-hand. Economic growth is the key to avoiding the kind of painful austerity that would limit America's ability to exercise both hard and soft power.

Today, some in this country relish the idea of America's retreat from her role in the world. They say that it's about time for other nations to take over; that America should turn inward; that she should recede from her unquestioned ability to defeat any foe.

Instead of heeding these calls for retreat, policymakers must renew their commitment to the idea that America is the greatest force for human freedom the world has ever seen; a country whose devotion to free enterprise has lifted more people out of poverty than any economic system ever designed; and a nation whose best days still lie ahead of it, if policymakers make the necessary choices today.

The Solution: Providing for the Common Defense

•	**Provide $554 billion for national defense spending in FY2013, an amount that is consistent with America's military goals and strategies.**

- **Reprioritize sequester savings to protect the nation's security.**

  The budget resolution offered by House Republicans ensures that the men and women who each day risk their lives in defense of the nation will continue to have the best training, equipment and support. This budget is not, however, a blank check for the military. To the contrary, this budget builds on the FY2012 budget's call for greater efficiency in the spending of defense dollars. Last year, the budget reduced the defense program by $78 billion over ten years to capture savings from the efficiencies identified under the leadership of secretary Gates. This year, another $60 billion of identified efficiencies are devoted to mission-critical defense priorities, including savings recommended by secretary Panetta.

  This budget resolution ensures that the base defense budget will not be cut during wartime. The President's defense budget request is 2.5 percent lower in real inflation-adjusted dollars than what Congress provided for this year. The House Republican budget provides level funding for defense so that the military has adequate funds to accommodate higher-than-anticipated fuel prices, to maintain training and readiness, and to keep faith with America's soldiers, sailors, airmen, and marines.

  Over the ten-year period covered by the budget resolution, this budget restores about half of the funding cut by the President and ensures that the defense budget grows in real terms in each year - providing adequate funding to maintain a robust end-strength and to address the years of forgone equipment modernization.

[7] "Analysis of the President's Budget for FY 2013,' U.S. House Budget Committee, February 24, 2012.
http:iibudget.house.goviUploadedFilesiPOTUs.FY13budget.pdf

Congress has no higher responsibility than to ensure that the President has available all the tools necessary to protect the national security. This budget meets that responsibility.

RESTORING ECONOMIC FREEDOM

The free enterprise system is being stifled by an epidemic of crony politics and government overreach that has weakened confidence in the nation's institutions and its economy.

This budget gets Washington out of the business of picking winners and losers, and restores fiscal discipline with over $5 trillion in cuts to government spending so the private sector can grow.

This budget repeals the President's health care law - curbing the federal government's overreach into personal health care decisions - and instead moves toward patient-centered reforms.

This budget reverses the President's policies that drive up gas prices, and instead promotes an all-of-the-above strategy for unlocking American energy production to help lower costs, create jobs and reduce dependence on foreign oil.

This budget unwinds government control over the housing giants, Fannie Mae and Freddie Mac, so they no longer expose taxpayers to trillions of dollars' worth of risk.

This budget revisits flawed financial-reform regulations and eliminates provisions that make future bailouts of Wall Street insiders more likely.

RESTORING ECONOMIC FREEDOM

The Challenge: A More Bureaucratic and Less Free America

For decades, the U.S. economy has been a magnet for investors, entrepreneurs and workers because America enjoys some of the strongest and most transparent legal protections in the world. These protections provide a stable environment for business investment - stability that is undermined when the discretionary power of bureaucrats is enhanced.

The United States still enjoys an enormous edge over most of the world when it comes to the strength of its institutions and its respect for the rule of law. But America is moving in the wrong direction, and job creators have taken notice.

In too many areas of the economy - especially energy, housing, finance, and health care - free enterprise has given way to government control in "partnership' with a few large or politically well-connected companies, and the rule of law is being replaced by the whims of politicians. The economy will not grow to its potential until government restores certainty and confidence by eliminating the cronyism that inevitably results when government assumes the power to pick winners and losers through its taxing, spending, and regulatory might.

Energy

The President's energy policies have been characterized by punitive regulations on economically competitive sources of energy, coupled with reckless spending on uncompetitive alternatives. Even in the midst of failed stimulus outcomes, the administration presented another budget this year with yet another energy stimulus program. The President's FY2013 budget would increase energy spending government-wide, including both discretionary and mandatory spending, by almost 90 percent over last year's enacted levels, and 138 percent over FY2011.

Since the introduction of this failed energy policy in the 2009 stimulus bill, the Department of Energy (DOE) has issued $20 billion in new loan guarantees for renewable energy projects. The most notorious of these - solar start-up Solyndra - received a loan guarantee for $535 million in the fall of 2009, even after repeated warnings from federal financial analysts about the firm's financial shakiness.
Meanwhile, advocates of green energy have argued that it's not enough for the government to subsidize alternatives - it should also promote policies that make commercially competitive sources of energy more expensive. Then-candidate Obama agreed, arguing in January of 2008: "Under my plan of a cap and trade system, electricity rates would necessarily skyrocket.'[8]

This was the idea behind the controversial "cap and trade' bill that President Obama tried and failed to pass through Congress in 2009, which would have established an elaborate bureaucratic structure for taxing and rationing conventional energy sources. But instead of accepting this verdict on its preferred policy, the administration continued to pursue de facto cap and trade approaches by supporting the Environmental Protection Agency's (EPA) unilateral plan to impose emissions restrictions on American businesses.

The push by the Obama administration to pursue energy and environmental policy through heavy-handed regulations circumvents accountability to voters and leaves decisions in the hands of a bureaucratic infrastructure. Unnecessary regulations tie the hands of small businesses and create a hostile and uncertain business environment, discouraging job growth.

*Senator Barack Obama, *San Francisco Chronicle* editorial board meeting, January 17, 2008.
http:iiwww.sfgate.comicgi-biniobjectiarticle?f=iciai2008io1i2oiEDIAUHAsH.DTL&o=0

In some areas, such as fuel-economy standards, the administration has abused a rulemaking process in order to ensure compliance from private-sector parties - for instance, bailing out General Motors and Chrysler as it was telling them to accept government's more costly fuel-economy standards.[9]
In other areas, such as the debate over the new Keystone pipeline, the administration has simply blocked action that would result in more jobs and lower energy prices for Americans. President Obama has chosen to delay a decision on this common-sense job creator until after the next election, despite years of vetting and an exhaustion of inadequate excuses.[10]

The result: since the start of the administration, gas prices have doubled; regulations have extracted almost $2 trillion per year from the economy, according the small Business Administration, including $281 billion for environmental regulations imposed on small businesses; and government "investments' have failed.[11]

Fannie Mae and Freddie Mac

The federal takeover of Fannie Mae and Freddie Mac continues to be the most costly taxpayer bailout to result from the 2008 financial crisis. So far, Fannie and Freddie have received over $185 billion in taxpayer-funded bailouts.[12]

For years, policymakers insisted that Fannie and Freddie, despite being government-sponsored enterprises (GsEs), posed no liability to the federal government. Through their unique status, which they cultivated through political influence, they recklessly expanded their balance sheets, privatized their profits, outsourced their risks to the American public, and created a disaster for taxpayers.

Taxpayers' exposure to Fannie and Freddie, once an implicit guarantee, has now become an explicit obligation to cover its debts. While under conservatorship, CBO estimates that Fannie and Freddie could cost taxpayers an all-in $335 billion. In contrast, the administration's proposed budget does not fully account for the taxpayer exposure of Fannie and Freddie, choosing instead to leave them off-budget.

Despite the government's abysmal track record of interference in the housing market, Fannie, Freddie, and another government housing agency, the Federal Housing Administration, now dominate 97 percent of the market for the issuance of new mortgage-backed securities. Corporate-welfare arrangements like the GsEs socialize risk by shifting losses to the taxpayers, but allow profits to accrue to management, bondholders and Wall Street institutions that trade mortgage-backed securities. On their current course, the GsEs represent a failed experiment in corporate welfare and the largest bailout of financial institutions in recent history.

Financial Services

The actions taken at the height of the financial panic of 2008, with credit markets frozen, succeeded in halting a systemic panic, but the Troubled Asset Relief Program (TARP) has since morphed into crony capitalism at its worst. Abandoning TARP's original and limited purpose of providing targeted assistance to unlock credit markets, the Treasury Department's senior officials transformed TARP into an ad hoc, opaque bailout and a slush fund for large private institutions.

° For more details, see the discussion of the automaker bailouts later in this chapter. " "Waiting for the Keystone XL Pipeline,' House Energy and Commerce Committee, accessed March 3, 2012. http:iienergycommerce.house.govikeystonexl.shtml " "The Empty Promise of Green Jobs,' House Budget Committee, September 22, 2011.
http:iibudget.house.goviNewsiDocumentsingle.aspx?DocumentID=261226

"Committee on Financial services, Views and Estimates of the Committee on Financial services on Matters to be set Forth in the Concurrent Resolution on the Budget for Fiscal Year 2013. March 6, 2012.

TARP was supposed to be confined to a narrow emergency. Unfortunately, the use of TARP funds was approved for the bailouts of all sorts, including cash infusions for the automakers General Motors and Chrysler. This entrenched the idea that TARP could be used for just about any kind of economic intervention, regardless of the fact that the original bill charged the program only to, quote, "purchase. Troubled assets from any financial institution.' Even greater damage came later, when the Obama administration used the auto bailout to trample the rights of Chrysler's secured bondholders - including state pension funds - in order to give politically favored groups a better deal than they were entitled to under the bankruptcy law. The damage done by the automaker bailouts went well beyond reducing confidence in the U.S. bankruptcy system - it was on display when the administration used unbalanced closed-door meetings to strong-arm automakers into supporting new fuel-economy regulations.[13]

The financial-regulation law authored in 2010 by Senator Chris Dodd and Representative Barney Frank (the Dodd-Frank Act) offers another example of the trend of government overreach in the private sector. The Dodd-Frank Act has expanded the power of unelected bureaucrats, created a mandate for hundreds of new regulations, and entrenched the role of influence-peddlers in Washington. It has solidified government's guarantee of Wall Street at the expense of the taxpayer and imposed burdensome compliance costs on a wide array of private-sector companies. Although the bill is dubbed "Wall street Reform,' it actually intensifies the problem of too-big-to-fail by giving large, interconnected financial institutions advantages that small firms will not enjoy.

While the authors of the Dodd-Frank Act went to great lengths to denounce bailouts, this law only sustains them. The Federal Deposit Insurance Corporation (FDIC) now has the authority to draw on taxpayer dollars to bail out the creditors of large, "systemically significant' financial institutions. CBO's expected cost for this new authority is $33 billion, although the office recognizes that "the cost of the program will depend on future economic and financial events that are inherently unpredictable.'[14] In other words, another large-scale financial crisis in which creditors are guaranteed to get government bailouts would cost taxpayers much, much more.

Developments in the area of financial-services regulation, including the Dodd-Frank Act, amount to an enormous transfer of power to the same bureaucrats who were blindsided by the financial meltdown of 2008. This will further deter economic expansion, invite political corruption and degrade self-government.

Health Care

The President's health care law is the crown jewel of the new crony politics. The law increases the discretionary power of bureaucrats, which in turn increases the power of those special interests in the health care industry that are big enough to secure themselves a seat at the table when the rules are written. The law as written guarantees over $800 billion in subsidies for health insurance companies by subsidizing the purchase of government-approved health insurance and forcing people to buy it.[15]

The cronyism in the new law does not stop at the transfer of billions of taxpayer dollars to the insurance industry. It also allows the Health and Human services secretary and federal bureaucrats to grant waivers exempting favored groups from its onerous mandates. For a lucky few, such as the many unions that have been granted waivers, this amounts to a "stay' from the full consequences of the new law. For the unlucky many without political connections, this means subservience to the whims of the party in power - even if First Amendment rights to religious liberty are involved, as America's religious employers have recently learned the hard way.

^vDarrell Issa, Chairman of the House Committee on Oversight and Government Reform, to Kathryn Ruemmler, Counsel to the President, February 29, 2012.

http:iioversight.house.goviimagesistoriesiLettersi2012-02-29 DEI to Ruemmler-WH - CAFE standards due 3-14.pdf

ⁱⁱ Douglas M. Elmendorf, statement Before the subcommittee on Oversight and Investigations, Review of CBO's Cost Estimate for the Dodd-Frank Wall street Reform and Consumer Protection Act, March 30, 2011.

^{ix} "Updated Estimates for the Insurance Coverage Provisions of the Affordable Care Act,' Congressional Budget Office, March 2012.

http:iiwww.cbo.govisitesidefaultiflesicboflesiattachmentsio3-13-Coverage%20Estimates.pdf

Though the right to freedom of conscience has not been respected in the waiver process, the administration has for other reasons granted over 1,400 businesses and organizations temporary waivers from the law's requirements.ⁱⁱ These waivers do not guarantee permanent relief, nor do they help those firms that lack the connections to lobby for waivers. The powerful discretion assumed by the administration to play judge in determining who receives these waivers and whether or not to extend them does tremendous damage to the rule of law.

The health care law vastly expands an already unwieldy administrative state, creating 159 new boards, bureaucracies, commissions and government programs.ⁱⁱ The law is built around the assumption that bureaucrats, if given enough power over the health care marketplace, can curb rising health care costs by expertly determining prices and dictating treatment options to doctors and patients. This "fatal conceit' stands in stark contrast to America's historic commitment to individual liberty and personal responsibility. In the health care sector as elsewhere, the best way to control costs is to give Americans control over the money they spend on health services, thus letting bottom-up competition driven by 300 million consumers control costs, improve quality and expand access.

The approach represented by the new law transforms the relationship between citizen and state, leaving individuals increasingly passive and dependent on their government. It will substantially diminish quality of and access to care as future policymakers cut costs to meet budgetary bottom lines rather than patients' medical needs. There is no way for "experts' in Washington to know more about the health care needs of individual Americans than those individuals and their doctors know, nor should they second-guess how each individual would prioritize services against costs.

The new health care law has taken the nation a giant step closer to a fully socialized system. The problems with this approach are already popping up all over the country. Health care costs are escalating relentlessly. The new law has aggravated the worst aspects of the U.S. health care system, without fixing what was (and remains) broken.

The Choice: Cronyism and Corporate Welfare vs. A Level Playing Field

In each major sector of the economy, the President and his party's leaders have offered a vision at odds with the core principles of economic freedom. It is an obsolete vision that favors big, well-established or politically well-connected corporations and unions at the expense of workers and small competitors. It is a vision that creates political inequality by favoring companies with the best connections over those with the best ideas. And it is a vision that inhibits growth by increasing the cost of complying with government regulations instead of leaving enterprises with more money and more freedom to hire workers and create jobs.

America's leaders must offer a new vision for a new century - not by applying old tax-and-spend policies to whatever industrial fad is popular in Washington, but by freeing the small businessperson, the worker and the entrepreneur to keep writing the American success story.

Cronyism and Corporate Welfare

In energy, the President and his party's leaders remain committed to a policy that blocks proven domestic energy sources while spending recklessly on uncompetitive alternatives.

In housing, the administration has failed to take action to account honestly for the liabilities of Fannie Mae and Freddie Mac, and it continues the bailout of these entities that has already cost taxpayers hundreds of billions.

In financial services, the President and his party's leaders remain wedded to an approach that views the consolidation of big banks - and the empowerment of the same regulators who failed to see the last crisis coming - as "reform,' when it is actually an invitation to corruption and potentially greater financial collapse down the road.

[16] "Annual Limits Policy: Protecting Consumers, Maintaining Options, and Building a Bridge to 2014,' Centers for Medicare and Medicaid studies.
http:iiccio.cms.goviresourcesiflesiapproved applications for waiver.html

[17] "159 Ways the senate Bill is a Government Takeover of Health Care.' senate Republican Policy Committee, February 25, 2010. http:iiwww.gop.goviblogi10i02i25i159-ways-the-senate-bill.

And in health care, the administration continues to transform one-sixth of the U.S. economy into a government-directed industry, rife with bureaucratic favoritism and capricious rules that trample the liberties of individuals, families, churches, non-profits, and employers.
In addition to these interventions, the President and his party's leaders continue to overstep government's bounds by punishing businesses in order to reward the organized-labor groups that finance their campaigns. The actions of the National Labor Relations Board (NLRB) under this administration offer another good example of bureaucratic overreach and the decline of the rule of law. The most notorious case involves Boeing, which the NLRB sued over its decision to locate a new factory in South Carolina instead of union-friendly Washington State. The Board's actions threatened hundreds of jobs. Eventually the NLRB dropped its lawsuit at the request of the politically connected union that had prompted the suit.[18]

By picking winners and losers in the market, the government-as-investor model distorts markets, subverts the rule of law, and fails to spur sustainable job creation. Instead of helping the economy, billions of taxpayers' dollars are thrown away, successful companies are deprived of their competitive advantages, and workers lose their jobs.

This is the ugly end of government's failed experiment with crony capitalism. Fortunately, there is a better way forward.

A Level Playing Field

Restoring the rule of law - reducing the influence of bureaucrats in the lives of Americans and empowering individuals instead - is central to the reforms proposed in this budget. In fact, such reforms go hand in hand with efforts to lift the crushing burden of debt, secure the social safety net, spur job creation, and restore economic growth for all.

In energy, Congress must limit the EPA's discretionary power to impose a bureaucratic version of the job-destroying cap-and-trade program, and it must allow the private sector to develop proven sources of American-made energy, creating jobs and lowering the price of energy here at home.

In housing, Congress must put an end to the practice of corporate welfare and taxpayer bailouts, especially by winding down government guarantees and ending taxpayer subsidies for Fannie and Freddie.

In financial services, Congress needs to reassert democratic control over unaccountable bureaucrats and establish a regulatory environment that is fair, neutral, predictable, and reasonable, with reforms that foster growth and responsibility; ensure that credit can be efficiently accessed by families and entrepreneurs; and hold to account those who violate the rules.

And in health care, Congress must repeal the President's disastrous new law, diminish the power of unelected bureaucrats over personal health care decisions, and restore that power to individuals and families by advancing reforms that allow robust choice and competition in health care.

Regarding organized labor, Congress needs to protect the economic freedom and security of working Americans by reining in the NLRB, a federal agency that is threatening job creation by overreaching its mandate. Because a majority of union members in the United States now works for the public sector, organized labor has become an increasingly powerful force on behalf of bigger government and higher taxes.[19] Policymakers must make sure America has a public sector that works for the people it serves - not the other way around.

[18] Steven Greenhouse, "Labor Board Drops Case Against Boeing After Union Reaches Accord,' New York Times, December 9, 2011.
http:iiwww.nytimes.comi2011i12i10ibusinessilabor-board-drops-case-against-boeing.html

[19] Catherine Rampell, "In Unions, Government Workers surpass Private-sector Workers,' *Economix* (blog), *New York Times*, January 22, 2010.
http:iieconomix.blogs.nytimes.comi2010i01i22iin-unions-government-workers-surpass-private-sector-workersi

The Solution: Restoring Free Enterprise
Ending Cronyism and Corporate Welfare

- **Restore competition and exploration as the keys to a vibrant energy sector, and get the government out of the business of picking winners and losers.**

  In stark contrast to the President's energy policy, this budget promotes new energy exploration to discover unknown energy resources, generate millions of new high-paying jobs and help fund needed infrastructure initiatives.

  This budget would continue funding essential government missions, including energy security and basic research and development, while paring back duplicative spending and non-core functions, such as applied and commercial research or development projects best left to the private sector. And it would immediately terminate all programs that allow government to play venture capitalist with taxpayers' money.

  It scales back spending on government bureaucracies that are seeking to impose a job-destroying national energy tax. It assumes increased revenues from bonus bids, rents, royalties, and fees as a result of lifting moratoriums and bans on safe, environmentally responsible exploration for domestic energy supplies. And it allows private development of all American-made energy, including nuclear, wind and solar.

  Ultimately, the best energy policy is one that encourages robust competition and innovation to ensure the American people an affordable and stable supply of energy. This budget would roll back federal intervention and expensive corporate welfare funding directed to favored industries. Instead, it would promote policies aimed at reliable energy, lower energy prices, greater revenue generation through prosperity, and market-based solutions for sustainable energy.

• **Privatize the business of government-owned housing giants, Fannie Mae and Freddie Mac, so they no longer expose taxpayers to trillions of dollars' worth of risk.**

This budget will put an end to the practice of corporate welfare and taxpayer bailouts in housing finance. It proposes eventual elimination of Fannie Mae and Freddie Mac, winding down their government guarantees and ending taxpayer subsidies. It supports various mechanisms intended to bring back private capital, shrink the GsEs' retained portfolios, and increase transparency and accountability. One option for scaling back the GsE's overreach would be to cap the value of a home for which Fannie or Freddie could guarantee a loan. Such a policy would reduce the number of loans the entities could back, naturally shrinking their market share.

The housing-finance system of the future will allow private-market secondary lenders to fairly, freely and transparently compete, with the knowledge that they will ultimately bear appropriate risk for the loans they guarantee. Their viability and profitability will be determined, not by political favoritism, but by the soundness of their practices and the value of their services.

• **Reform the Credit Reform Act to stop the transfer of taxpayer risk to FHA.**

As the bailouts of Fannie and Freddie continue, another bailout to a housing giant looms. The FHA's Mutual Mortgage Insurance Fund's capital reserve ratio has fallen to 0.24 percent - far below its congressionally-mandated level of 2 percent. Should the capital ratio fall below zero, yet another taxpayer bailout of a housing finance giant will be automatically triggered.[20]

[20] Committee on Financial services, Views and Estimates of the Committee on Financial services on Matters to be set Forth in the Concurrent Resolution on the Budget for Fiscal Year 2013. March 6, 2012.

Given the precarious financial position of the FHA, the government should adopt measures to discourage shifting of taxpayer risk to the FHA and other government-backed entities as Fannie and Freddie are wound down. The current budgetary treatment of FHA loans understates the full costs associated with them, thus it encourages policymakers to shift risk from Fannie and Freddie to FHA. This budget calls for the use of fair-value scoring for federal credit programs. Without it, the full risk of FHA loans - effectively borne by taxpayers - cannot be properly accounted for in the budget.

• **Revisit flawed financial-reform regulations and eliminate provisions that make future bailouts more likely.**

This budget would end the bailout regime enshrined into law by the Dodd-Frank Act. The federal government has a critical role in helping to ensure financial markets are fair and transparent, and in holding accountable those who violate the rules. But even though that role is critical, it is a limited one: Federal bureaucrats should not be empowered to micromanage the financial system, and this budget will review financial regulations to ensure that the costs to the private sector and to the taxpayer do not outweigh their benefits, and that regulations are both essential and not unduly burdensome.

Future reforms should aim to restore the principles that have made American capital markets the envy of the world: freedom to participate, an unbreakable link between performance and reward, full accountability for risk, avoidance of moral hazard, and a sense of responsibility that ensures that those who seek to reap the gains also bear the full risk of losses.

- **Repeal the President's health care law.**

    This budget would put an end to the cronyism and corporate welfare created by government overreach into the health care sector. What America already knows about the law is this: Costs are going up, premiums are rising, and millions of people will lose the coverage they currently have. Job creation is being stifled by its taxes, penalties, mandates and fees.

    The President's new health care law will exacerbate the spiraling cost of health care, explode deficits and debt, and forever alter the relationship between the government and the American people. Repealing the exchange subsidies stops this downward slide and saves roughly $808 billion over the next ten years by abolishing the government spending and making sure that not a penny goes toward implementing the new law.

    This repeal turns of the new gusher of taxpayer money for those special interests that were powerful enough to ensure themselves a seat at the table when the 2,700 page law was being written. It also stops the invasive mandates from bureaucrats who grant waivers to the privileged and impose one-size-fits-all regulation on the rest.

- **Move toward patient-centered reform.**

    There is a consensus of willing leaders from both parties coalescing around the right way forward in health care. Reform should address government-imposed inequities and barriers to true choice and competition. Commonsense solutions include enacting medical liability reform, ensuring Americans can purchase quality coverage across state lines, and expanding access to consumer-directed health care options. Addressing distortions in the tax code could begin by giving employers the opportunity to offer their employees a free choice option, so that workers could be free to devote their employer's health coverage contribution to the purchase a health insurance plan that works best for them.

    - **Boost private-sector employment by slowing the growth of the public sector, achieving a 10 percent reduction over the next three years in the federal workforce through attrition, coupled with a pay freeze until 2015 and reforms to government workers' fringe benefits.**
    The federal government has added 147,000 new workers since the President took office. It is no coincidence that private-sector employment continues to grow only sluggishly while the government expands: To pay for the public sector's growth, Washington must immediately tax the private sector or else borrow and impose taxes later to pay down the debt.

    The federal government's responsibilities require a strong federal workforce. Federal workers deserve to be compensated equitably for their important work, but their pay levels, pay increases and fringe benefits should be reformed to better align with those of their private-sector counterparts.

    Compensation for federal workers continues to outpace pay for their private-sector counterparts. The non-partisan CBO recently released a study saying that federal workers are, on average, compensated 16 percent higher than comparable private-sector employees.[21] Immune from the effects of the recession, federal workers have received regular salary bumps regardless of productivity or economic realities.

    The reforms called for in this budget aim to slow the federal government's unsustainable growth and reflect the growing frustration of workers across the country at the privileged rules enjoyed by government employees. They reduce the public-sector bureaucracy, not through layoffs, but via a gradual, sensible attrition policy. By 2015, this reform would result in a 10 percent reduction in the federal workforce.

Additionally, this budget freezes federal pay through 2015 and asks federal employees to make a more equitable contribution to their retirement plans. When combined, these proposals will save taxpayers approximately $368 billion over ten years.

Cutting Spending So the Economy Can Grow

• **Build on continued efforts to pare back spending on government bureaucracies by capping spending.**

Whether branded as stimulus or rebranded as investment, government spending is no substitute for a true recovery led by the private sector. All of this borrowed money and debt is fueling uncertainty for businesses and job creators, who know that today's deficits are tomorrow's interest rate and tax increases.

Getting spending under control is critical. This budget builds on the efforts achieved under the Budget Control Act to cap spending. It would achieve spending reduction, not just through across-the-board cuts, but by scaling back funding for agencies whose recent budgetary increases have fueled the epidemic of crony politics and government overreach that has weakened confidence in the nation's institutions and its economy.

• **Take action to eliminate wasteful Washington spending, building upon the suggestions of the President's Fiscal Commission, the work of the House majority, and the proposals put forward by an array of non-partisan, independent watchdogs that have worked to expose the abuse of taxpayer dollars.**

Washington's spending problem did not just develop in the last few years. It will require even more work to undo the damage of decades of reckless spending increases. This budget restores fiscal discipline to government. It does this, not through indiscriminate cuts, but by compelling the elimination of dozens of wasteful and duplicative programs identified by non-partisan watchdogs and government auditors.

[^] "Comparing Benefits and Total Compensation in the Federal Government and the Private sector,' Congressional Budget Office, January 30, 2012.
http://iiwww.cbo.govisitesidefaultiflesicboflesiftpdocsi126xxidoc12696i01-30-FedPay.pdf

Anti-Fraud Accounts: The federal government wastes billions of American taxpayers' dollars each year by making improper payments to individuals, organizations and contractors. In 2011 alone, the federal government made an estimated $115 billion in improper payments. This budget funds targeted increases in anti-fraud accounts, saving billions of dollars in waste, fraud, and abuse in the Medicare, Medicaid, supplemental security Income, and Disability Insurance programs.

Sales of Unneeded Federal Assets: In the last year alone, Republicans put forth proposals to sell unneeded federal property. Representative Jason Chafetz has proposed to sell millions of acres of unneeded federal land. Likewise, Representative Jef Denham's bill to authorize the sale of billions of dollars worth of federal assets would save the government money, collect corresponding revenue, and remove economic distortions by reducing public ownership. Such sales could also potentially be encouraged by reducing appropriations to various agencies. If done correctly, taxpayers could recoup billions of dollars from selling unused government property.

This budget proposes to reduce the federal auto feet (excluding the Department of Defense and the U.s. Postal service) by 20 percent; streamline the process and rationalize the regulations for the disposal and sale of federal property to eliminate red tape and waste; set enforceable targets for asset sales; and hold government agencies accountable for the buildings they oversee.

Government Accountability Office (GAO) recommendations: Each year GAO issues a report on eliminating duplicative government programs and saving taxpayers money. In its 2012 report, GAO identified dozens of examples of waste, duplication and overlap.[22] Comptroller General of the United States, Gene Dodaro, recently testified that implementing the suggested reforms government-wide "could potentially save tens of billions of dollars."[23]

This budget proposes that all authorizing committees (which oversee government departments and agencies) should annually provide to the House Budget Committee (which writes the budget) spending reduction recommendations for programs in their jurisdictions that are duplicative, wasteful, outmoded, or excessively expensive for the benefits received. Furthermore, these recommendations should be made publicly available, so that taxpayers are provided with the transparency required for full accountability in government.

Other examples of wasteful spending: This budget doesn't just take the recommendations of others - it draws upon House Budget Committee examinations that combed the federal budget for other examples of wasteful spending. While no federal department is free of inefficiency, the Department of Transportation in particular offered a number of areas where spending could be cut back responsibly.

In the first two years of the Obama administration, funding for the Department of Transportation grew by 24 percent - and that doesn't count the stimulus spike, which nearly doubled transportation spending in one year. The mechanisms of federal highway and transit spending have become distorted, leading to imprudent, irresponsible, and often downright wasteful spending. Further, however worthy some highway projects might be, their capacity as job creators has been vastly oversold, as demonstrated by the extravagant but unfulfilled promises that accompanied the 2009 stimulus bill, particularly with regard to high-speed rail.

In the wake of these failures, and with the federal government's fiscal challenges making long-term subsidization infeasible, high-speed rail and other new intercity rail projects should be pursued only if they can be established as self-supporting commercial services. The threat of large, endless subsidies is precisely the reason governors across the country are rejecting federally-funded high-speed rail projects. This budget eliminates these projects, which have failed numerous and clear cost-benefit analyses.

[22] 2012 Annual Report: Overlap and Fragmentation, Achieve Savings, and Enhance Revenue, U.S. Government Accountability Office, March 2012.
http:iiwww.gao.goviproductsiGAO-12-342sP

[23] Gene L. Dodaro, Testimony before the U.S. House Oversight Committee, Government 2.0: GAO Unveils New Duplicative Program Report, February 28, 2012.
http:iioversight.house.govihearingigovernment-2-0-gao-unveils-new-duplicative-program-reporti

• **Reflect the economic reality of record-high farm income by restructuring farm programs, saving taxpayers money and increasing farmer independence.**

Compared to an overall economy that is recovering slowly, the American agricultural sector is improving dramatically. The record-breaking prosperity of American farmers and farm communities is to be celebrated. But it also calls for a re-examination of federal agricultural programs that spend billions each year. Taxpayers should not finance payments for a business sector that is more than capable of thriving on its own.

Net farm income this year is forecast to be modestly lower than last year's very high level, but it would still be the third highest inflation-adjusted income level recorded since 1980.[24] Production costs have risen, but farmer incomes continue to be supported by strong prices for most crop and livestock commodities. The top five earnings years for farmers in the last 35 years have occurred in the last decade. Yet, at the same time, numerous overlapping government programs exist to provide income support to farmers.

With farm profitability - and deficits - continuing at high levels, it is time to adjust support to this industry to reflect economic realities. This budget proposes two major reforms to achieve this: First, reduce the fixed payments that go to farmers irrespective of price levels, to reflect that soaring commodity prices are reducing the need for high levels of farm-income support. Second, reform the open-ended nature of the government's support for crop insurance, so that agricultural producers assume the same kind of responsibility for managing risk that other businesses do.

Recognizing that the Agriculture Committee is responsible for implementing these reductions, and to maintain flexibility for the Agriculture Committee, this proposal assumes that these savings do not take effect until the beginning of the next farm bill. These reforms will save taxpayers roughly $30 billion over the next decade. " "Farm Income and Costs: 2012 Farm sector Income Forecast,' U.s. Department of Agriculture, Economic Research service, accessed March 19, 2012.

http:iiwww.ers.usda.goviBriefngiFarmIncomeinationalestimates.htm

REPAIRING THE SOCIAL SAFETY NET

KEY POINTS

The unsustainable government programs aimed to bolster the social safety net are failing to deliver on their promise to society's most vulnerable citizens.

The skewed incentives of federal safety-net programs foster dependence and leave lower-income Americans most at risk to consequences of the looming spending-driven debt crisis.

This budget repairs the safety net by returning power over public-assistance programs to the states, directing assistance to those who need it most, and strengthening federal education and job-training programs to help Americans get back on their feet.

This budget gives states the freedom and flexibility to tailor a Medicaid program that fits the needs of their unique populations.

This budget better focuses other low-income assistance programs, including food stamps, to those that need them most, realigning incentives to ensure these programs can best meet their critical missions.

This budget ensures higher-education assistance programs are put on a sustainable funding path, better focusing aid on those in need and better addressing the root drivers of tuition inflation for all students.

This budget consolidates dozens of overlapping job-training programs into accountable career scholarships so that workers have the tools to thrive in the 21st century global economy.

REPAIRING THE SOCIAL SAFETY NET

The Challenge: A Safety Net in Danger of Unraveling

The recent downturn has imposed great economic hardship upon millions of Americans. Beyond the tumult of the recent recession and weak recovery, there has been increasing anxiety for working families amidst rapid changes in the global economy. Technological advancement and the information revolution have fostered tremendous productivity gains, yet these have often come at the expense of dislocation for those working in the most-affected industries.

Government policies have imposed additional barriers to success on lower-income Americans. Failing schools have widened achievement gaps, and rising health care costs have eroded the value of paychecks. And some aspects of the safety net impose barriers of their own. For instance, the elimination of certain benefits as income rises has the effect of imposing a tax that discourages some low-income Americans from seeking lives of independence and self-sufficiency.

Republicans, Democrats and independents all believe in a sturdy safety net for those who, through no fault of their own, have fallen on hard times. The debate is over how best to strengthen and improve it. In particular, it is essential to prevent benefit structures from becoming barriers to upward mobility.

The safety-net system created in the last century is in dire need of a new round of reform. Government programs that aim to support the safety net are failing the citizens who rely on them and the taxpayers who fund them. A system designed for mid-20th century demographics and economics is ill equipped to deal with the unique pressures of the 21st century.

From a budgetary perspective, these programs are growing at an unsustainable rate. The recent economic downturn greatly increased the eligibility and the demand for government assistance programs. Yet even prior to the 2008 financial crisis, and controlling for economic performance, there has been a dramatic increase in government spending on public assistance programs. Medicaid spending grows, on average, 9 percent a year - far faster than the growth of the overall economy. And federal spending on food stamps has quadrupled over the past ten years. Unless reforms are enacted to put these programs on sustainable footing, these skyrocketing rates of spending will threaten the safety net with a debt crisis that leads to forced austerity.

From a moral perspective, while well-intentioned, the paternalistic structures of these programs fail the very people they are intended to help. Many of these government programs - designed by distant government agencies, financed through outdated government formulas, and administered by unresponsive government bureaucrats - are slow to adjust to the changing needs of unique communities. Worse, government's expansive reach too often undermines nongovernmental institutions better suited to assist individuals in need, because it substitutes federal power in their place. Government programs should bolster - not displace - the family, civic and religious institutions that serve communities across the nation.

The strains that many of these well-intentioned programs have placed on the nation have reached a breaking point.

Medicaid

Medicaid, the program created 50 years ago to provide health care coverage for the poor, is coming apart at the seams. The open-ended nature of the program's current financing structure has created rapidly rising costs that are nearly impossible to check. In 1966, the first year of the program's operation, total costs were $400 million. By

2009, the total cost of administering Medicaid had soared to $378.6 *billion*. Absent fundamental reform, total annual costs are expected to continue climbing and reach a total of $804 billion by 2019[25].

[25]Centers for Medicare and Medicaid services, "2012 Actuarial Report on the Financial Outlook for Medicaid' Office of the Actuary, December 21, 2010. p.19.
http:iiwww.cms.goviActuarialstudiesidownloadsiMedicaidReport2010.pdf

Moreover, much of this spending is wasted, because the bureaucracy cannot provide adequate oversight of this open-ended program. Medicaid's improper payment rate is over 10 percent, more than three times the amount of waste that other federal agencies generate. This translates into a combined $33 billion worth of waste each year.[26] Medicaid's current structure gives states a perverse incentive to grow the program and little incentive to save. The federal government pays an average of 57 cents of every dollar spent on Medicaid.[27] Expanding Medicaid coverage during boom years can be tempting for state governments since they pay less than half the cost. Conversely, to restrain Medicaid's growth, states trying to rescind a dollar's worth of coverage only save themselves 43 cents.[28]

Moreover, states are not given adequate flexibility to achieve savings, even though many governors have asked for a new approach.[29] Instead, one-size-fits-all federal mandates don't permit innovative coverage options, and many times the only way states are allowed to achieve savings is through formulaic cuts to medical providers. Many doctors are refusing to treat Medicaid patients, because states have reduced their reimbursements below what it costs to treat them.[30]

Doctors who still see Medicaid patients at below-market reimbursement rates are forced to shift their loss to non-Medicaid patients, contributing in effect to the health cost inflation that is currently putting quality, affordable health coverage out-of-reach for an increasing number of Americans.[31]

As a shared program between the states and the federal government, the program's unsustainable growth is putting enormous stress on both federal and state balance sheets. CBO estimates that federal spending on Medicaid will grow from nearly $276 billion in 2013 and to nearly $622 billion over the next ten years. This translates into an annual growth rate of 9 percent over that period.[32] should policymakers continue to ignore this problem, two outcomes are inevitable: significant cuts in benefits that will restrict access and massive tax increases that will stifle growth.

All Americans will pay more because this Medicaid system has broken down - and not just in higher taxes. Because Medicaid's reimbursement rates have been ratcheted down to below-market levels, the quality of care that Medicaid patients receive is declining below standard. Recent studies have indicated that Medicaid patients are more likely to die after coronary artery bypass surgery, less likely to get standard care for blocked heart arteries, and more likely to die from treatable cancer, than those with other coverage options.[33] By some measures, such as in-hospital death rates following major surgeries, Medicaid patients fared even worse than the uninsured.[34]

[26] Government Accountability Office, "Improper Payments: Progress Made but Challenges Remain in Estimating and Reducing Improper Payments,' GAO-09-628T, April 22, 2009, p. 12. http:iiwww.gao.goviassetsi130i122319.pdf

[27] Department of Health and Human services, "Financing and Reimbursement', Medicaid.gov.
http:iiwww.medicaid.goviMedicaid-CHIP-Program-InformationiBy-TopicsiFinancing-and-ReimbursementiFinancing-and-Reimbursement.html

[28] Ibid. [29]*A New Medicaid: A Flexible, Innovative and Accountable Future, Republican Governors Public Policy Committee,*

Health Care Task Force, August 30, 2011.

http:iirgppc.comirgppc-medicaid-reporti

[31] Kevin sack, "As Medicaid Payments shrink, Patients Are Abandoned,' *New York Times*, March 15, 2010.
http:iiwww.nytimes.comi2010i03i16ihealthipolicyi16medicaid.html

[32] Doug Rapp, "Low Medicare, Medicaid Pay Rates Impact Private Costs.' *American Medical News*, January 5, 2009.
http:iiwww.ama-assn.orgiamednewsi2009i01i05igvsb0105.htm

[33]Congressional Budget Office, "Medicaid spending and Enrollment Detail for CBO's March 2012 Baseline.' March 13, 2012. http:iiwww.cbo.govisitesidefaultiflesi cboflesiattachmentsi43059 Medicaid.pdf

[34]Scott Gottlieb, M.D., "Medicaid Is Worse Than No Coverage at All.' *Wall Street Journal*, March 10, 2011. [35] Ibid.

Medicaid has fostered an unfair two-class system within the health care marketplace that stigmatizes Medicaid enrollees, and its perverse funding structure is exacerbating budget pressures at the state and federal level, while creating a mountain of waste. With administrators looking to control costs and providers refusing to participate in a system that severely under-reimburses their services, Medicaid beneficiaries are left on their own to navigate an increasingly complex system for even the most basic procedures. Absent reform, Medicaid will not be able to deliver on its promise to provide a sturdy health care safety net for society's most vulnerable.

Supplemental Nutrition Assistance Program (Food Stamps)

The supplemental Nutritional Assistance Program (sNAP, formerly known as food stamps) serves an important role in the safety net by providing food aid to low-income Americans. But this program cannot continue to grow at its current rates. The cost has exploded in the last decade, from less than $18 billion in 2001 to over $80 billion today. As recently as 2007, sNAP was projected to cost slightly less than $400 billion over ten years. Currently, the ten-year projection has risen to almost $772 billion.

Much of this is due to the recession, but not all of it: Enrollment grew from 17.3 million recipients in 2001, to 23.8 million in 2004, to 28.2 million in 2008, to 46.6 million today. According the U.s. Department of Agriculture, "The historical relationship between unemployment and sNAP caseloads diverged in the middle of the decade. As the unemployment rate fell 1.4 percentage points between 2003 and 2007, sNAP caseloads increased by 22 percent.'[35] The trend is one of relentless and unsustainable growth in good years and bad. The large recession-driven spike came on top of very large increases that occurred during years of economic growth, when the number of recipients should have fallen.

This unsustainable cost growth is the result of the same flawed structure that has fueled unsustainable growth in Medicaid. State governments receive federal dollars in proportion to how many people they enroll in the program, which gives them an incentive to add more individuals to the rolls. State governments have little incentive to make sure that able-bodied adults on sNAP are working, looking for work, or enrolled in job training programs.

This leads to a program rife with waste, fraud and abuse. In the past year, Michigan has had *two* lottery winners continue to receive sNAP benefits.[36] In New York, former and current New York City employees created false names, addresses and social security numbers to create approximately 1,500 false sNAP cards.[37] These individuals netted $8 million. And, under the leadership of Chairman Darrell Issa, the House Oversight Committee has uncovered dozens of additional examples of abuse, such as recipients collaborating with vendors to trade food stamps for cash, cigarettes and alcohol.[38] This kind of abuse must stop. By providing states with incentives to reduce fraud and abuse, the federal government can ensure its sNAP dollars address hunger and malnutrition in the United States without lining the pockets of criminals.

Education and Job Training

Globalization and technological advances have made the modern economy more complex and dynamic. The new reality is workers at all levels must be ready to update or learn new, more specialized skills to match the changing needs of employers competing in the global economy. Federal higher education and job-training programs must be reformed to help workers adapt to this new challenge.

[36] Margaret Andrews and David Smallwood, "What's Behind the Rise in sNAP Participation,' *Amber Waves*, March, 2012. http:iiwww.ers.usda.goviAmberWavesiMarch12iFeaturesisNAPRise.htm

[37] Ed White, "Lottery winner. Food stamps. In Michigan. Aqain,' *Associated Press*, March 9, 2012. http:iiwww.csmonitor.comiBusinessiLatest-News-Wiresi2012i0309iLottery-winner.-Food-stamps.-In-Michigan.-Again

[38] Colin Moynihan, "Four Charged With stealing $8 Million in Food stamp scam,' *New York Times*, December 8, 2010. http:iiwww.nytimes.comi2010i12i09inyregioni09hra.html

[39] Darrell Issa, Chairman of the House Committee on Oversight and Government Reform, to Tom Vilsack, secretary of Agriculture, February 6, 2012. http:iioversight.house.goviwp-contentiuploadsi2012i03i2012-02-06 DEI to Vilsack-USDA - sNAP program due 2-21.pdf

Current federal aid structures are exacerbating a crisis in tuition inflation, plunging students and their families into unaffordable levels of debt or foreclosing the possibility of any higher education at all. This problem has been building for years and has officially reached crisis levels. In June 2010, student loan debt surpassed the national level of credit card debt for the first time in history. The graduating class of 2011 is the most indebted to date, with an average per student debt of $22,900.[39]
These young adults are graduating with enormous loan repayments and having difficulty finding jobs in our low-growth economic environment. Instead of solving the problem, schools are defecting the mounting criticism by blaming the rising cost of health care and employee benefits, the need to compete for students by offering nicer facilities, and reductions in state subsidies and endowments as a result of the recession.[40] While these do represent contributing factors, they are merely accelerating a long-standing problem. College costs have risen at twice the rate of inflation for about thirty years, but this year fees soared 8.3 percent - more than double the inflation rate - as federal subsidies have increased at a historic pace.[41]

But, instead of helping more students achieve their dreams, studies have shown that increased federal financial aid is simply being absorbed by tuition increases. While financial aid is intended to make college more affordable, there is growing evidence that it has had the opposite effect. Economists such as Richard Vedder point out that the decisions of colleges and universities to raise their prices would have been constrained if the federal government had not stepped in so often to subsidize rising tuitions.[42]

When it comes to job training and continuing education, the current policy landscape is dotted with failed, unaccountable and duplicative programs. There are at least 49 such programs spread across nine agencies, costing up to $18 billion annually.

A 2011 Government Accountability Office (GAO) report found that almost all federal employment and training programs overlap one or more similar programs, providing similar services to similar populations, and only five of these programs have ever been evaluated for effectiveness. Beyond the ineffectiveness and duplication, senators Coburn and McCain issued a report in February 2011 that highlights the numerous examples of waste, fraud and abuse that this system has become known for.[43]

The Successful Example of Welfare Reform

Empowerment is a powerful alternative to dependency, and recent history offers a guide to policymakers seeking to repair the safety net. Bipartisan efforts in the late 1990s transformed cash welfare by encouraging work, limiting the duration of benefits, and giving states more control over the money being spent. Opponents of these policy changes argued that welfare reform would lead to large increases in poverty and despair.

Instead, the opposite occurred. The Temporary Assistance for Needy Families (TANF) reforms cut welfare caseloads in half as poverty rates declined. In stark contrast to critics' fears, child-poverty rates fell 1 percent per year in the five years following the passage of TANF in 1996.

[39] Mark Whitehouse, "Number of the Week: Class of 2011, Most Indebted Ever,' *Real Time Economics* (blog), *Wall Street Journal*, May 7, 2011.
http:iiblogs.wsj.comieconomicsi2011i05i07inumber-of-the-week-class-of-2011-most-indebted-everi

[40] Jane V.Wellman, statement before the House subcommittee on Higher Education and Training, *Keeping College Within Reach*, November 30, 2011.
http:iiedworkforce.house.goviUploadedFilesi11.30.11 wellman.pdf

[41] Patrick M. Callan, "College Affordability: Colleges, states Increase Financial Burdens on students and Families,' *Measuring Up.*
http:iimeasuringup.highereducation.orgicommentaryicollegeafordability.cfm

[42] Dr. Richard K. Vedder, remarks before the House Committee on Education and the Workforce, *College Access: Is Government Part of the Solution, Or Part of the Problem?* April 19, 2005. http:iiwww.gpo.govifdsysipkgiCHRG-109hhrg20645ihtmliCHRG-109hhrg20645.htm

[43] senator Tom A. Coburn, "Help Wanted: How Federal Job Training Programs Are Failing Workers,' February, 2011.
http:iiwww.coburn.senate.govipubliciindex.cfm?a=Files.serve&File id=9f1e1249-a5cd-42aa-9f84-269463c51a7d

These reforms worked because the best welfare program is temporary and ends with a job and a stable, independent life for the beneficiary. At the federal level, the successful welfare-reform movement of the 1990s was narrowly focused on cash welfare payments. Based on the lessons learned from welfare reform, now is the time to implement similar reforms across other areas of the social safety net, especially Medicaid, sNAP and other programs that have not been significantly reformed since they were created.

If government is to require able-bodied recipients of aid to find work, as it should, then it must also help them return to productive working lives. To that end, federal education and job-training programs need to be modernized to keep the workforce competitive in a 21st-century, global economy. Government must do a better job of targeting resources to make sure that America's workforce can successfully pursue new opportunities and adopt new skills, if necessary.

The Choice: Greater Dependency vs. Upward Mobility

The President and his party's leaders have taken an approach to public assistance that encourages greater dependency and weakens community sources of support. The better approach is to remove barriers to upward mobility, so that all Americans have the opportunity to rise.

Greater Dependency

The President's top-down approach reveals a misguided view of the proper role for the federal government in building community bonds, extending the ladder of opportunity to all, and strengthening the nation's safety net.

His policies place trust in an empowered federal government in place of families, local communities, and faith-based groups, sapping the latter of vitality and weakening communities in the process. This has disastrous consequences for the most vulnerable Americans. Centralized bureaucracy is no substitute for a vibrant civil society in which citizens help each other on a personal basis.

The President's policies also reveal why the current structure of public assistance programs is unsustainable. The health care law, for example, is propelling the Medicaid crisis to a reckoning by forcing an additional 20 million Americans by 2019 into a system that can hardly handle its current enrollment.

The same flawed incentives distorting Medicaid have also exploded the cost of the sNAP program. Like Medicaid, the states administer the sNAP program, but unlike Medicaid, the entire cost of benefits under the sNAP program is born by the federal taxpayer. And this administration has managed to make a bad incentive structure worse. The 2009 stimulus bill included additional funding to states if they achieved higher enrollment levels. Unsurprisingly, food-stamp use is up by 46 percent since January 2009. Total spending has more than doubled in four years.[44]

The first two years of this administration were marked by a reckless expansion of the federal government's obsolete approach to education and job training, endangering the viability of advanced education services for those most in need. The administration's budget pushes Pell Grant spending toward unsustainable rates, contributing to tuition inflation and inhibiting upward mobility and access to better opportunities.

Instead of proposing a sensible consolidation of the complex web of job-training programs, the administration has sought to layer on new government programs, regardless of whether those programs are training workers for in-demand occupations. For example, the Labor Department Inspector General's latest audit reveals that new job-training programs specializing in "green" skills, funded by $500 million in stimulus funds, resulted in a mere 2 percent of trainees placed in jobs by these programs being retained more than six months.[45]

[44] Alan Bjerga and Jennifer Oldham, "Gingrich Calling Obama 'Food stamp President' Draws Critics,' *Bloomberg Businessweek*, January 25, 2012.
http:iiwww.businessweek.cominewsi2012-01-25igingrich-calling-obama-food-stamp-president-draws-critics.html

[45] Darrell Issa, Chairman of the House Committee on Oversight and Government Reform, to Hilda Solis, secretary of Labor, January 20,2012.
http:iioversight.house.goviimagesistoriesiLettersi2012-01-20 DEI to Solis-DOL - Green Jobs Program due 2-1.pdf

Upward Mobility

Poverty can never be reduced in the absence of a growing economy that produces jobs and facilitates shared prosperity. No economic system in the history of mankind has done more to lift up the poor than America's commitment to free enterprise. If the American Idea of earning success through work and enterprise is to endure through the 21st century, policymakers must urgently enact reforms to get Washington's fiscal house in order, spur job creation and promote sustained economic growth.

Beyond the urgent need to lift the crushing burden of debt and advance pro-growth reforms that spur sustained job creation, policymakers must reform public assistance programs to be more responsive, sustainable, and empowering to their beneficiaries. Government can play a positive role with policies that help the less fortunate get back on their feet and offer low-income Americans the opportunity to gain control over their lives.

•   The key to the welfare reform of the late 1990s was Congress's decision to grant states the ability to design their own systems. Congress should grant them the same flexibility with regard to Medicaid.

•   Congress should extend the successes of welfare reform to all assistance programs aimed at empowering lower-income Americans by implementing reforms that give states more flexibility to meet the needs of low-income populations and to make sure that the truly needy receive the assistance they need to live meaningful, independent lives.

•   Imposing time limits and work requirements on federal need-based aid is a positive reform. But education programs must be accountable and job-training programs must be effective so that vulnerable citizens can take advantage of them.

Above all, the role of policymakers must be to lift government-imposed barriers to stronger communities and flourishing lives. Fiscal responsibility and economic opportunity are but means to a more critical end: the rebuilding of broken communities and the empowerment of families and citizens. The ever-expansive activism of the federal government drains the vitality and displaces the primacy of the bedrock institutions that define America.

The Solution: Repairing the Social Safety Net

Repairing a Broken Medicaid System

•   **Secure Medicaid benefits by converting the federal share of Medicaid spending into a block grant indexed for inflation and population growth. This reform ends the misguided one-size-fits-all approach that has tied the hands of so many state governments. States will no longer be shackled by federally determined program requirements and enrollment criteria. Instead, they will have the freedom and flexibility to tailor Medicaid programs that fit the needs of their unique populations.**

•   **Improve the health care safety net for low-income Americans by giving states the ability to offer their Medicaid beneficiaries more options and better access to care. Medicaid recipients, like all Americans, deserve to choose their own doctors and make their own health care decisions, instead of having Washington dictate those decisions to them.**

Protecting Assistance for Those in Need

- **Constraining Medicaid's growing cost trajectory by $810 billion over ten years, contributing to the long-term stability of the federal government's fiscal condition and easing the largest and fastest growing burden on state budgets.** Medicaid provides a revealing case study in how structural flaws in government health care programs are harming the very people these programs are meant to assist. In response both to budget constraints imposed by Medicaid's growth and policy constraints imposed by numerous federal mandates, state governments systematically underpay doctors and hospitals - making across-the-board cuts to a one-size-fits-all program instead of implementing smart reforms that allow states to carefully tailor benefits. As a result, doctors and nurses are fleeing the system to escape endless red tape and underpayments. Meanwhile, beneficiaries are left with fewer provider choices and reduced access to care.

Worse, the one-size-fits-all mandates Washington forces on states have almost eliminated local government's flexibility to manage care in their communities. This has led to lower quality care, restricted access, and financial trade-offs that leave beneficiaries and taxpayers worse off.

Offering states more flexibility for their Medicaid beneficiaries will remove the stigma recipients face and allow them to take advantage of a range of options. Several of the nation's governors have made innovative proposals to fix Medicaid. This budget pursues reforms in this direction.

- **Convert the Supplemental Nutrition Assistance Program (SNAP) into a block grant tailored for each state's low-income population, indexed for inflation and eligibility beginning in 2016 - after employment has recovered. Make aid contingent on work or job training.**

- **Begin devolving other low-income assistance programs to the states. State governments can better tailor assistance programs to their specific populations, providing a more robust safety net and reducing waste in these programs.**

With regard to federal low-income assistance programs, starting with sNAP, this budget proposes two of the reforms that led to the success of welfare reform in the late 1990s.

First, the budget ends the flawed incentive structure that rewards states for signing up ever-higher numbers of recipients. By capping the open-ended federal subsidy and freeing states to come up with innovative approaches to delivering aid to those who truly need it, this reform encourages states to reduce rolls and help recipients find work.

Second, it calls for time limits and work requirements like those that proved successful at cutting welfare rolls in half and reducing poverty nationwide. These changes would be phased in gradually, however, to give states and recipients opportunity to adjust and the employment time to recover.

Preparing the Workforce for a 21st Century Economy

- **Reform the Credit Reform Act to reflect the true cost of federal student-loan programs that are driving up the cost of tuition.**

In 2010, the government went from primarily guaranteeing private student loans to lending 100 percent of its student-loan money directly through the Department of Education, turning the agency into one of the largest lending banks in the country. These student loan funds have to be borrowed from global credit markets at an average of at least $100 billion per year, adding to already dangerous federal debt levels. Even more problematic, according to outdated current scoring rules, these extremely risky loans appear as profit-making investments in the federal government's books, thus encouraging more loan expansion, even though there is evidence that subsidized lending contributes to tuition inflation.

Accounting for market risk in the scoring of these programs would simultaneously reflect their true cost to taxpayers and make risky expansions of these programs less likely to occur. To that end, this budget authorizes the use of fair-value accounting principles for any legislation dealing with federal loan and loan-guarantee programs.[46]

- **Return Pell Grants to a sustainable funding path to ensure aid is available for the truly needy and to curb tuition inflation for all students.**

Even the President's budget acknowledges that college costs are on an unsustainable path. Furthermore, recent studies have demonstrated that increases in Pell Grants appear to be matched nearly one for one by increases in tuition at private universities.[47] This budget puts Pell on a sustainable path by limiting the growth of financial aid and focusing it on low-income students who need it the most. This will force schools to reform and adapt. It will also ensure that Pell spending goes to students who truly need it.

Moreover, federal intervention in higher education should increasingly be focused not solely on financial aid, but on policies that maximize innovation and ensure a robust menu of institutional options from which students and their families are able to choose. Such policies should include reexamining the data made available to students to make certain they are armed with information that will assist them in making their postsecondary decisions. Additionally, the federal government should act to remove regulatory barriers in higher education that act to restrict flexibility and innovative teaching, particularly as it relates to non-traditional models such as online coursework.

• **Consolidate dozens of overlapping job-training programs into accountable career scholarships to improve access to career development assistance and strengthen the first rung on the ladder out of poverty.**

This budget advances reforms to increase job-training outcomes across the board. It builds on past improvements, as well as legislation recently introduced by Republican members of the Education and the Workforce Committee under the leadership of Chairman John Kline.[48] It improves accountability by calling for the consolidation of duplicative federal job-training programs into a streamlined workforce development system with fewer funding streams that provide accountable, targeted career scholarship programs. Instead of wasting job-training money on duplicative administrative bureaucracy, this budget calls for job-training programs to be better coordinated with each other - and with the Pell program - to maximize every dollar for those who need it.

This budget advances improved oversight and accountability for job-training programs and the Pell program by tracking the type of training provided, the cost per student, employment after training, and whether or not trainees are working in the field for which they were trained. These programs should also track beneficiaries' participation levels in federal support programs (e.g., welfare and sNAP) before and up to five years after training to determine if the training led to self-sufficiency. These common-sense measures will enable policymakers to determine whether private and non-profit institutions are training beneficiaries effectively.

---

[46] For more detail, see "Reform the Credit Reform Act to incorporate Fair Value accounting principles' in the *Changing Washington's Culture of Spending* chapter of this report.

[47] Larry D. Singell, Jr., and Joe A. stone. "For Whom the Pell Tolls: The Response of University Tuition to Federal Grants-in-Aid.' Oregon University, September, 2005.
http:iipages.uoregon.eduilsingelliPell Bennett.pdf

[48] "H.R. 3610, the streamlining Workforce Development Programs Act' House Education and Workforce Committee, December 8, 2011.
http:iiedworkforce.house.goviNewsiDocumentsingle.aspx?DocumentID=271811

STRENGTHENING HEALTH AND RETIREMENT SECURITY

KEY POINTS

- ☑ The future of the nation's health and retirement security programs is increasingly based on empty promises from a government unwilling to advance solutions that save and strengthen them.

- ☑ This budget strengthens health and retirement security by taking power away from government bureaucrats and empowering patients with control over their care.

- ☑ This budget repeals the new health care law's unaccountable board of bureaucrats empowered to cut Medicare in ways that would jeopardize seniors' access to care.

- ☑ This budget saves Medicare for current and future generations, with no disruptions for those in and near retirement.

- ☑ For younger workers, when they become eligible, Medicare will provide a premium-support payment and a list of guaranteed coverage options – including a traditional fee-for-service option – from which recipients can choose a plan that best suits their needs.

- ☑ Program growth would be determined by a competitive bidding process – with choice and competition forcing providers to reduce costs and improve quality for seniors.

- ☑ Premium support, competitive bidding, and more assistance for those with lower incomes or greater health care needs will ensure guaranteed affordability for all seniors.

- ☑ This budget also establishes a mechanism that requires action by the President and leaders in Congress to shore up Social Security's fiscal imbalance.

STRENGTHENING HEALTH AND RETIREMENT SECURITY

The Challenge: Empty Promises Turning Into Broken Promises

Over the past century, the federal government has forged a social contract with working families to furnish a strong and stable base of health and retirement security for America's seniors. Medicare is a critical program that helps seniors to achieve health security. Social security delivers a minimum level of income security for retirees, those with disabilities, and survivors.

But the failure of politicians in Washington to be honest about Medicare and social security is putting the health and retirement security of all Americans at risk. The fact is that Medicare and social security are in dire need of reform if these 20th century programs will be able to deliver on their promise in the 21st century. With both programs weighed down by tens of trillions of dollars of unfunded liabilities, the federal government is making promises to current workers about their health and retirement security for which it has no means to pay. Without reform, these empty promises will soon become broken promises.

Washington's policy response to the demographic and economic pressures threatening Medicare and social security has been a disappointing failure. For too long, politicians of both parties have lacked the political will to deal with the underlying structural issues that are weakening these programs. Instead, they have denied the problem or made the problem worse.

- In Medicare, government has tried and failed to address cost pressures by cutting provider payments in ways that hurt quality and restrict access for seniors. Absent reform, current seniors will experience diminished care, while the next generation will inherit a bankrupt Medicare program.

- In social security, government's refusal to deal with demographic realities has endangered the solvency of this critical program. Absent reform, seniors, those with disabilities, and their families will experience sharp benefit cuts when the trust fund is exhausted in 2036, while the next generation will inherit a social security program too unstable to permit them to plan for their own retirement with confidence.

Unfortunately, years of neglect by policymakers who were unwilling to confront the structural challenges posed by these programs are pushing Medicare and social security into a state of peril. Left unaddressed, the spending pressures in these programs don't just put the solvency of the federal government at risk and future economic growth in doubt -they also threaten the government's ability to protect the promise of health and retirement security for millions of seniors today, as well as for generations to come.

Medicare

With the creation of Medicare in 1965, the United States made a commitment to help fund the medical care of elderly Americans without exhausting their life savings or the assets and incomes of their working children and younger relatives. In urging the creation of Medicare, President Kennedy said that such a program was chiefly needed to protect people who had worked for years and suddenly found all their savings gone because of a costly health problem.[49]

Medicare's disastrous structural imbalance puts this mission at risk, as beneficiaries' access to quality, affordable care will be severely restricted if Medicare is left on its present course. Unless Congress fixes what's broken in

Medicare, without breaking what's working, the program will end up causing what it was created to avoid - millions of American seniors without adequate health security and a younger working generation saddled with enormous debts to pay for spending commitments that cannot be sustained.

[49] President John F. Kennedy, *Address at a New York Rally in Support of the President's Program of Medical Care for the Aged*, May 20, 1962.

The current Medicare program attempts to do two things to make sure that all seniors have secure, affordable health insurance that works. First, recognizing that seniors need extra protection when it comes to health coverage, it pools risk among all seniors to ensure that they enjoy secure access to care.
Second, Medicare subsidizes coverage for seniors to ensure that coverage is affordable. Affordability is a critical goal, but the subsidy structure of Medicare is fundamentally broken and drives costs in the wrong direction. The open-ended, blank-check nature of the Medicare subsidy drives health care inflation at an astonishing pace, threatens the solvency of this critical program, and creates inexcusable levels of waste in the system.

Politicians' repeated failures to solve this problem underscore the critical need for structural reform to ensure lasting solvency. Time and again, Congress has applied band-aids to control costs by reducing the rate at which doctors, hospitals and other providers are reimbursed for treating Medicare patients.

These repeated fee reductions create backwards incentives for those providing care, resulting in the volume of services provided for each condition being increased, costs being shifted onto private health insurance plans, or Medicare patients simply losing access to care. The incentive to increase volume results in waste, fraud and abuse. The incentive to shift costs results in higher costs for all patients. And the incentive to turn Medicare patients away results in restricted access to critical care for seniors.

Medicare alone is currently projected to rise from 3.7 percent of GDP to 14 percent of GDP by 2085. But according to CBO, the trust fund that sustains Medicare will run out of money long before that - a mere ten years from now. The unchecked growth of the Medicare program cannot be sustained, and the government's continued reliance on price controls will only make matters worse. Washington's failure to advance structural reforms threatens not just the affordability of coverage for seniors, but also the security that comes with knowing that coverage can be obtained at any price.

Social Security

In the words of President Franklin D. Roosevelt, social security was created to provide an antidote to the "dreadful consequence of economic insecurity' for the elderly and for vulnerable citizens in times of need.[50] The program is financed through a pay-as-you-go system, which means that current workers' social security taxes are used to pay benefits for current retirees. In 1935 when social security was enacted, there were about 42 working-age Americans for each retiree. The average life expectancy at birth for men in America was 60 years; for women it was 64.

The demographic situation has changed dramatically, however, since the creation of the program. This evolution in the demographic composition of the U.S. population was accompanied by the enactment of large expansions in eligibility for benefits and of taxes to finance those benefits. In 1950, there were 2.9 million beneficiaries. Currently, there are over 55 million beneficiaries - an eighteen-fold increase.[51] When the program was created, workers and their employers each paid a 1 percent payroll tax. Today, they each pay a 6.2 percent payroll tax.

The explosion of payments in the 75 years since the social security system was enacted will be dwarfed by the demographic demands of the very near future. The first members of the baby-boom generation - those born between 1946 and 1964 - are already eligible for early retirement. At the same time, thanks to innovations in medical technology and health care, life expectancies have lengthened to an average 75.9 years for men and 80.6 years for women, and are expected to grow further. This unquestionably positive development requires policymakers to respond with reforms that ensure that this 20th-Century program can make good on its promise in the 21st Century.

Not only is the nation aging, but there has also been a demographic shift to a lower retirement age. In 1945, the average age of retirement was 69.6 years. In 2009, it was 63.8 years.

[*] President Franklin D. Roosevelt, Message to Congress on social security, January 17, 1935.
http:iiwww.ssa.govihistoryifdrstmts.html

[9] "2011 OsADI Trustees Report,' U.s. social security Administration, May 13, 2011. http:iiwww.ssa.govioactiTRi2011iindex.html

To put this in perspective: when social security was first enacted in 1935, each worker, on average, was contributing less than 2.5 percent of one retiree's benefits. By 2030, each wage earner will be paying for nearly *half* of each retired person's full benefits.
This represents a massive shift of earnings away from younger families trying to build for their futures, toward social security recipients. No economy can grow and thrive under that heavy a tax burden.

Those who wish to solve this problem by raising taxes often ignore the economic damage that such large tax increases would entail. Just lifting the cap on income subject to social security taxes, as some have proposed, would, when combined with the Obama administration's other preferred tax policies, lift the top marginal tax rate to over 50 percent. Despite having a limited direct impact on the solvency of the program, these tax increases would impose adverse consequences to retirement security programs by weakening their most critical source of funding: a growing, prosperous economy.

Most economists agree that raising marginal tax rates that high would create a significant drag on economic growth, job creation, productivity and wages. This nation cannot fix its retirement-security system by leaving young families with nothing to save.

If the nation acts now, those in and near retirement can enjoy the continuity of health and retirement arrangements around which they have organized their lives. If Washington continues to play politics with the future of these programs, however, then it won't just be future generations at risk: Current retirees will also find their benefits subject to a significant reduction of 23 percent when the social security trust funds are no longer able to pay full benefits.

Empty promises

Policymakers have known about these problems in Medicare and social security for decades, but few have been willing to propose real solutions. Yet each year that Congress fails to act, the U.S. government gets closer to breaking promises to current retirees while adding to a growing pile of empty promises made to future generations.

America has seen unfunded obligations much, much less severe than these take down some of its proudest companies. In industries such as steel, aviation and autos, workers lost promised benefits when their employers failed to take timely, responsible steps to update their unworkable, 20th-century benefit structures. Many workers lost their jobs, while retirees lost the critical health and retirement benefits that they were counting on.

Unless Congress acts, Americans can expect the same thing to happen to social security and Medicare. Trustee

Reports over the past decades, signed by presidential appointees of both parties, have urged policymakers to act. The added strain from the severe recession has had the same effect on Medicare and social security as experienced by the private sector. Medicare is on a similarly unsustainable path - the Medicare trend line illustrated in Figure 4 is an economic impossibility. Future benefit cuts - against a backdrop of skyrocketing costs - are a certainty if the program goes unreformed.

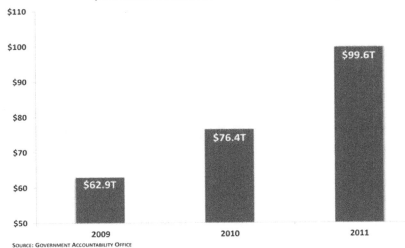

FIGURE 3

THE COST OF WAITING – THE FISCAL GAP
(UNFUNDED PROMISES IN TRILLIONS OF DOLLARS)

SOURCE: GOVERNMENT ACCOUNTABILITY OFFICE

Americans have enough instability in their lives, and they deserve a federal health and retirement safety net that they can count on. If Congress wants to avoid defaulting on federal health and retirement programs, it must adopt a program of gradual adjustment now -one that frees the nation from the shadow of debt, strengthens its health and retirement safety net, protects those in or near retirement from any disruptions in their benefits, and supports robust economic growth and job creation.

Otherwise, the nation will face more significant, unpopular, and immediate overhauls later. As Stephen Goss, Chief Actuary of the social security Administration, put it in a House Budget Committee hearing this year, "Our trustees and everybody who speaks on this has opined extensively about the value of acting sooner rather than later, so that we can have gradual changes phased in and we have more options if we act relatively soon.'[52]

The Choice: Bankruptcy and Denied Care vs. Strength and Solvency

The demographic and economic drivers of the nation's debt are well known, and there is little disagreement about the nature of the problem. But there is a profound disagreement about the right approach to dealing with these problems. One approach is to deny that these problems are embedded in the current system, rely on unelected and unaccountable bureaucrats to save money by restricting access to health care services, and chase ever-higher spending commitments with ever-higher tax increases. The other approach is characterized by a recognition that the problems are structural in nature, coupled with real reforms that adjust programs to demographic reality and use choice and competition to control costs and improve care for seniors.

Bankruptcy and Denied Care

The President's new health care law is emblematic of the wrong way to address the problems with Medicare. First, the overhaul raided Medicare by nearly $700 billion to fund a new, unsustainable, open-ended health care entitlement. Second, it created a government panel of bureaucrats with the power to impose price controls on providers in ways that would result in rationed care and restricted access to treatments. Meanwhile, with regard to social security, the President and his party's leaders continue to ignore the problem.

[5] Stephen Goss, Testimony before U.s. House Budget Committee, *Strengthening Health and Retirement Security*, February 28, 2012.
Raiding Medicare: The trillion-dollar overhaul of the U.S. health care sector enacted by the last Congress was filled with gimmicks and double-counting to hide its true cost.

Supporters claimed that it would *both* shore up the Medicare trust fund *and* offset the cost of the expensive new health care entitlement that the new law created.

The President himself announced that the new law "actually added at least a dozen years to the solvency of Medicare,' while also claiming that it wouldn't add to the deficit[53]. But at a House Budget Committee hearing last year, Medicare's chief actuary, Richard Foster, testified that it would be impossible for the new law to do both unless the savings were double-counted.

"Both will happen as a result of the same one set of savings, under Medicare," Foster explained. "But it takes two sets of money to make it happen. When we need the money to extend the Hospital Insurance Trust Fund, we have a promissory note. And Treasury has to pay that money back. But they have to get it from somewhere. That's the missing link."[54]

FIGURE 4

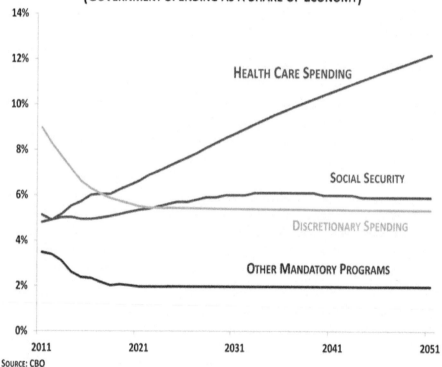

HEALTH CARE COSTS ARE THE PRIMARY DRIVER OF THE DEBT
(GOVERNMENT SPENDING AS A SHARE OF ECONOMY)

HEALTH CARE SPENDING

SOCIAL SECURITY

DISCRETIONARY SPENDING

OTHER MANDATORY PROGRAMS

SOURCE: CBO

The hard truth of the President's law is that it provided no mechanism for paying the money back - it simply raided Medicare to partially pay for its new entitlement.

Rationing Medicare: There are two ways to control health care spending: Give bureaucrats the power to decide which health care services seniors can use, as the Democrats' health care law will do starting in 2014, or give patients more power to reward providers who deliver high-quality, low-cost care (and deny business to those who fail to provide quality, affordable care), as Republicans seek to do.

The new health care law empowers bureaucrats at the expense of patients and providers, setting up an unelected board - the Independent Payment Advisory Board, or IPAB - tasked with cutting Medicare through formulaic rationing. One size-fits-all Washington-based decisions to restrict certain treatments punish beneficiaries by hitting all providers of the same treatment with across-the-board cuts, with no regard to measures of quality or patient satisfaction.

<u>Letting social security go Bankrupt:</u> The deny-and-delay approach to social security's looming bankruptcy was illustrated perfectly last year by senate Majority Leader Harry Reid of Nevada. First, Reid claimed that warnings of social security's bankruptcy represented "an outright lie.'[55] Then, when confronted with the trustees' report showing that social security's trust funds will be exhausted by 2036, Leader Reid replied, "Two decades from now, I'm willing to take a look at it. But I'm not willing to take a look at it right now.'[56]

Similarly, the top Democrat in the United States House of Representatives, House Minority Leader Nancy Pelosi of California, refuses to acknowledge social security's most basic math. When asked in 2006 when she would put forward a plan to fix social security, Pelosi responded: "Never. Is never good enough for you?'[57]

This combination of policies - raid, ration, raise taxes, and deny the problem - will mean painful benefit cuts for current seniors and huge tax increases on younger working families, robbing them of the opportunity to save for their own retirements. And it will mean that those pledges of future health and retirement security that the government is currently making to younger families are nothing but empty promises. Unless government acts, Medicare and social security will remain threatened for current seniors and will not be there for younger families.

[53] President Barack Obama. Weekly Address, Office of the Press secretary, The White House. August 7, 2010. http:iiwww.whitehouse.govithe-press-ofcei2010i08i07iweekly-address-president-obama-highlights-benefts-seniors-under-patient

[54] Richard Foster, Testimony before U.S. House Budget Committee, *The Fiscal Consequences of the New Healthcare Law,* January 26, 2011. http:iibudget.house.govihealthcareihearing1262011.htm

[55] Laura Litvan, "Deficit Deal May Fail if U.S. social security Cuts Included, Durbin says,' *Bloomberg,* March 28, 2011. http:iiwww.bloomberg.cominewsi2011-03-28idefcit-deal-would-fail-if-u-s-social-security-cuts-included-durbin-says.html

[56]Jennifer Rubin, "Harry Reid says No to social security Reform,' Right Turn (blog), *Washington Post,* March 17, 2011. http:iiwww.washingtonpost.comiblogsiright-turnipostiharry-reid-says-no-to-social-security-reformi2011i03i04iABtwgdk_blog.html

[57] Perry Bacon Jr., "Don't Mess With Nancy Pelosi,' *Time,* August 27, 2006. http:iiwww.time.comitimeiprintoutio,8816,1376213,00.html

Strength and Solvency

There is a better way forward - a way that accounts for both the benefits and the failures of these programs, and builds upon the good while reforming the bad.

There is a way to strengthen Medicare and save it from insolvency. Instead of using Washington-based price controls that simply pay providers less while jeopardizing seniors' care, there is a growing bipartisan consensus for real reforms designed to slow the growth of health care costs economy-wide by promoting true choice and competition. Empowering seniors, not bureaucrats, is the best way to save and strengthen Medicare.

Reform aimed to empower individuals - with a strengthened safety net for the poor and the sick - will not only ensure the fiscal sustainability of this program, the federal budget, and the U.S. economy. It will also guarantee that Medicare can fulfill the promise of health security for America's seniors.

There is also a way forward on social security that requires all parties to acknowledge the fiscal realities of this critical program.

It is morally unconscionable for elected leaders to cling to an unsustainable status quo with respect to America's

health and retirement security programs. Current seniors and future generations deserve better than empty promises and a diminished country. Current retirees deserve the benefits around which they organized their lives. Future generations deserve health and retirement security they can count on.

The Solution: Strengthening Health and Retirement Security

Saving and Strengthening Medicare

- **Save Medicare for current and future generations, with no disruptions for those in and near retirement.**

- **For younger workers, when they reach eligibility, Medicare will provide a Medicare payment and a list of guaranteed coverage options - including a traditional fee-for-service option - from which recipients can choose a plan that best suits their needs. These future Medicare beneficiaries will be able to choose a plan the same way members of Congress do. Medicare will provide additional assistance for lower-income beneficiaries and those with greater health care needs.**

To strengthen the Medicare program to serve the needs of both current and future retirees, the budget would reform the Medicare program and put it on sound financial footing for generations to come. For those workers currently under the age of 55, beginning in 2023, those seniors would be given a choice of private plans competing alongside the traditional fee-for-service option on a newly created Medicare Exchange. Medicare would provide a premium-support payment either to pay for or offset the premium of the plan chosen by the senior.

The Medicare Exchange would provide seniors with a competitive marketplace where they could choose a plan the same way members of Congress do. All plans, including the traditional fee-for-service option, would participate in an annual competitive bidding process to determine the dollar amount of the federal contribution seniors would use to purchase the coverage that best serves their medical needs. Health care plans would compete for the right to serve Medicare beneficiaries.

The second-least expensive approved plan *or* fee-for-service Medicare, whichever is least expensive, would establish the benchmark that determines the premium-support amount for the plan chosen by the senior. If a senior chose a costlier plan than the benchmark plan, he or she would be responsible for paying the difference between the premium subsidy and the monthly premium. Conversely, if that senior chose a plan that cost less than the benchmark, he or she would be given a rebate for the difference. Payments to plans would be risk-adjusted and geographically rated. Private health plans would be required to cover *at least* the actuarial equivalent of the benefit package provided by fee-for-service Medicare.

Program growth would be determined by the competitive bidding process - with choice and competition forcing providers to reduce costs and improve quality for seniors. The competitive market for Medicare choices would foster innovation and quality, while ensuring that the program is financially stable. In an exchange with Chairman Paul Ryan before the House Budget Committee, Medicare Chief Actuary Foster cited analysis and experience on the merits of competitive bidding as a promising means to improve quality and control costs in the Medicare program.[58]

As opposed to pegging the growth rate to a predetermined formula, competitive bidding offers the ideal means of harnessing the power of choice and competition to control costs, while also securing guaranteed affordability for patients. As a backup, the per capita cost of this reformed program for seniors reaching eligibility after 2023 could not exceed nominal GDP growth plus 0.5 percent.

The President has repeatedly proposed empowering IPAB to hold Medicare growth to the same growth rate. The difference is that this budget proposes to use competition to control costs, while IPAB under the President's proposals would use bureaucratic benefit restrictions (i.e., "value-based benefit design') to contain Medicare's growth to below GDP plus 0.5 percent.[59]

The cap on the growth rate is intended to: (1) act as a fallback to assure the federal government budgetary savings and protect the future of Medicare; and (2) foster the proper incentives for providers and plans to develop more efficient methods of quality care delivery and attract seniors to those plans that succeed.

This budget also seeks to strengthen protections for lower-income Americans. If costs rose faster than this established limit, those low-income individuals who qualify for both Medicare and Medicaid (also known as "dual-eligibles') would continue to have Medicaid pay for their out-of-pocket expenses. Other lower-income seniors (those who do not qualify for Medicaid but are still under a certain income threshold) would receive fully-funded accounts to help offset any out-of-pocket costs.

Guarantee Affordable Choices for All Seniors

Seniors would be guaranteed a plan that is at least the value of the traditional fee-for-service Medicare option. Health plans that participate alongside a traditional Medicare option in the Medicare Exchange would be required to offer insurance to *all* seniors - regardless of age and health status - thereby preventing insurers from cherry-picking only the healthiest seniors for coverage under their plans. These protections ensure that Medicare's sickest and highest-cost beneficiaries have access to affordable and quality coverage choices. The proposal requires all plans on the Exchange to include guaranteed issue (i.e., they cannot deny coverage based on pre-existing conditions) and community rating (i.e., they cannot impose prohibitively disparate costs on seniors) to ensure that seniors are able to choose an affordable health plan that works best for them - without fear of denial or discrimination.

Stronger Protections for Those with Greater Needs

The federal contribution to seniors' health plans would be risk-adjusted so that the sickest seniors are protected from high premiums as well as adverse selection from insurers. Building on the risk-adjustment tools currently used by the Centers for Medicare and Medicaid services (CMs), proper risk adjustment would ensure that seniors with the highest health costs would still be able to find an affordable plan. Federal contributions would be increased to account for a senior's health status and age.

[58] Richard Foster, remarks before the House Budget Committee, *Strengthening Health and Retirement Security*, February 28, 2012.

http:iibudget.house.goviNewsiDocumentsingle.aspx?DocumentID=282298 [59] "Analysis for the President's Budget For FY2013,' House Budget Committee, February 24, 2012. http:iibudget.house.goviUploadedFilesiPOTUs FY13budget.pdf

CMs would also conduct an annual risk review audit of all insurance plans participating in the Medicare Exchange. Insurance plans covering a higher-than-average number of *low-risk* seniors would pay a fee. Conversely, insurance plans covering a higher-than-average number of *high-risk* seniors would receive an incentive payment. The fees and incentive payments would flow internally through the same fund, so that payments to plans that cover high-cost patients would be funded wholly by the fees from plans that cover low-cost patients.

More Support for Low-Income Seniors and a Reduced Subsidy for High-Income Seniors

Low-income seniors shopping for coverage would be offered the same range of high-quality options offered to all other seniors. They would be guaranteed the ability to choose a traditional fee-for-service Medicare plan, or they could choose a private plan on the Medicare Exchange with a fully-funded account from which to pay premiums, co-pays and other out-of-pocket costs.

The high-income means-testing thresholds for the Parts B and D programs would apply to the new Medicare program, such that certain high-income seniors would pay an increased share of their premiums.

Using Choice and Competition to Save and Strengthen Medicare

For too long in the Medicare system, the federal government, not the patient, has been the customer - and the government has been a clumsy, ineffective steward of value. Controlling costs in an open-ended system has proved impossible to do without limiting access or sacrificing quality. In a vain attempt to get control of the waste in the system, Washington has made across-the-board payment reductions to providers without regard to quality or patient satisfaction. It hasn't worked. Costs have continued to grow, seniors continue to lose access to quality care, and the program remains on a path to bankruptcy. Absent reform, Medicare will be unable to meet the needs of current seniors or future generations.

In health care, as in any other economic arrangement, control of money is power. When it comes to controlling health care costs and saving the nation from bankruptcy, the question is: Who gets the power? One centralized federal government, or 50 million empowered seniors holding providers accountable in a true marketplace? Patient power will always serve the needs of the people far better than bureaucrats managing the decline of a government-run system on the verge of bankruptcy.

These reforms will guarantee that Medicare can fulfill the promise of seniors' health security for generations to come. Premium support, competitive bidding, and more help for those with lower incomes and greater health needs will ensure guaranteed affordability for future seniors.

- **Stop the raid on the Medicare trust fund that was going to be used to pay for the new health care law. Any current-law Medicare savings must go to saving Medicare, not the creation of new open-ended health care entitlements.**

This budget ends the raid on the Medicare trust fund that began with passage of the new health care law last year. It ensures that any potential savings in current law would go to shore up Medicare, not to pay for new entitlements. In addition to repealing the health care law's new rationing board and its unfunded long-term care entitlement, this budget stabilizes plan choices for current seniors.

Table 1

The Simple Truth about Medicare's Future

	Bureaucrat Control	Patient Control
Proposal	The President's partisan health care law creates an unaccountable board of 15 unelected bureaucrats - the so-called "Independent Payment Advisory Board' (IPAB) - empowered to cut Medicare in ways that will result in denied care and restricted access for seniors. The bureaucrat-imposed cuts threaten critical care for current seniors and fail to strengthen Medicare for future generations.	Bipartisan solutions to preserve the Medicare guarantee, offering guaranteed coverage option options to future seniors, regardless of pre-existing conditions or health history, financed by a premium-support payment adjusted to provide additional financial assistance to low-income and less-healthy seniors and less to the wealthy. The Medicare health plans, including a traditional Medicare option, would compete against each other to offer higher quality care at lower costs.
Ration care?	Yes. IPAB's unelected and unaccountable bureaucrats have the power to determine what "rationing health care' means, allowing them to cut Medicare in ways that harm seniors' access to providers and lead to the denial of critical care.	No. strips unaccountable Washington bureaucrats of their rationing power; puts patients in control of their health care decisions instead of government, and forces providers to compete for the right to serve seniors. All Medicare health plans are required to meet high standards of care.
Control Costs?	No. Cutting reimbursements only reduces access, while the true costs of care continue to grow.	Yes. Harnessing the power of choice and competition helps tackle the root drivers of health inflation that are bankrupting the current system.
Who is in control?	An unaccountable board of 15 unelected bureaucrats.	Patients and their doctors.
Protect benefits?	No. The President's latest budget proposes to give IPAB "additional tools' that would give it the power to change benefits in ways that restrict seniors. seniors are prohibited from legal appeals to IPAB's decisions.	Yes. Making no changes for current seniors, ensuring that traditional Medicare remains an option, and strengthening the program for future seniors access for protects the Medicare guarantee.
Current seniors	Exposed to the harmful consequences of IPAB.	No changes.
Solvent future?	No. Medicare's trust funds are exhausted, and the collapses into bankruptcy.	Yes. Medicare will be able to deliver on its critical program mission to seniors today and future generations.

- **Repeal the rationing board that would limit seniors' care.**

  This budget repeals IPAB, the unaccountable panel of 15 unelected bureaucrats empowered by the President's health care law to cut Medicare in ways that would lead to denied care for seniors. Choice and competition - not bureaucratic rationing - is the best way to contain costs in government health care programs while at the same time improving the quality of care.

- **Ensure that the cost of frivolous litigation is not passed on to consumers in the form of higher health care premiums by capping non-economic damages in medical liability lawsuits.**

This budget also achieves savings by advancing common-sense curbs on abusive and frivolous lawsuits. Medical lawsuits and excessive verdicts increase health care costs and result in reduced access to care. When mistakes happen, patients have a right to fair representation and fair compensation. But the current tort litigation system too often serves the interests of lawyers while driving up costs.

Advancing Social Security Reforms

- **Establish a requirement that in the event that the Social Security program is not sustainable, the President, in conjunction with the Board of Trustees, must submit a plan for restoring balance to the fund. The budget then requires congressional leaders in both the U.S. House of Representatives and U.S. Senate to put forward their best ideas as well.**

- **Move the conversation to solutions that save Social Security, thus providing the space to forge a bipartisan path forward and ensure that Social Security remains a key part of retirement security for the future.**

In a shared call for leadership, this budget calls for action on social security by requiring both the President and the Congress to put forward specific ideas and legislation to ensure the sustainable solvency of this critical program. Both parties must work together to chart a path forward on common-sense reforms, and this budget provides the nation's leaders with the tools to get there.

Previous proposals put forward by leading reformers offer guidance on where bipartisan consensus can be reached on strengthening social security. For example, the President's Fiscal Commission advanced solutions to ensure the solvency of social security.

The Commission suggested a more progressive benefit structure, with benefits for higher-income workers growing more slowly than those of workers with lower incomes who are more vulnerable to economic shocks in retirement. It also recommended reforms that take account of increases in longevity, to arrest the demographic problems that are undermining social security's finances.[60]

In addition, there is bipartisan consensus that social security reform should provide more help to those who fall below the poverty line after retirement as part of a reform that makes the program solvent. As part of a plan to strengthen the safety of the nation's most vulnerable citizens, lower-income seniors should receive more targeted assistance than those who have had ample opportunity to save for retirement.

While certain details of the Commission's social security proposals are of debatable merit, the Commission undoubtedly made positive steps forward on bipartisan solutions to strengthen social security. This budget builds upon the Commission's work, forcing action to solve this pressing problem by requiring the President and Congress to work together to advance solutions.

People are living longer. The baby boomers have begun to retire. Health care costs are skyrocketing. These are facts, and they require a better approach to renew the social contract.

This budget fulfills the mission of health and retirement security for all Americans by saving and strengthening existing programs through common-sense reforms. The solutions are clear; what remains in question is whether elected leaders have the resolve to save these programs.

[60] "The Moment of Truth,' The National Commission on Fiscal Responsibility and Reform,' December, 2010.

http:iiwww.fscalcommission.govisitesifscalcommission.goviflesidocumentsiTheMomentofTruth12 1 2010.pdf

PRO-GROWTH TAX REFORM

KEY POINTS

The tax code has become a broken maze of complexity and political favoritism, overgrown with special-interest loopholes and high marginal rates that stifle economic growth and job creation.

This budget reforms the broken tax code to spur job creation and economic opportunity by lowering rates, closing loopholes, and putting hardworking taxpayers ahead of special interests. The pro-growth reforms ensure the tax code is fair, simple, and competitive.

This budget consolidates the current six individual income tax brackets into just two low brackets of 10 and 25 percent and repeals the Alternative Minimum Tax.

This budget reduces the corporate rate to 25 percent and shifts from a "worldwide' system of taxation to a "territorial' tax system that puts American companies and their workers on a level playing field with foreign competitors.

This budget rejects the President's call to raise taxes. Instead, it broadens the tax base to maintain revenue growth at a level consistent with current tax policy and at a share of the economy consistent with historical norms of 18 to 19 percent in the following decades.

PRO-GROWTH TAX REFORM

The Challenge: A Burdensome and Uncompetitive Tax Code

A world-class tax system should be simple, fair and pro-growth. The U.S. tax code fails on all three counts.

The tax code is notoriously complex: Individuals, families and employers spend over six billion hours and over $160 billion a year trying to negotiate a labyrinth of deductions.[61]

The tax code is patently unfair: Many of the deductions and preferences in the system - which serve to narrow the tax base - were lobbied for and are mainly used by a relatively small group of mostly higher-income individuals.

And the tax code creates a drag on growth, because it is highly inefficient, uncompetitive and unpredictable.

The Complex Tax Code

When the modern tax code was established in 1913, it contained roughly 400 pages of laws and regulations. Since then, the federal tax code has grown dramatically and now stands at more than 70,000 pages. In the past ten years, there have been more than 4,400 changes to the code, or more than one per day.[62] Many of the major changes made to the tax code over the years involved carving out special preferences, exclusions, or deductions for various activities or groups. These special tax breaks and preferences now add up to more than $1 trillion per year. Both parties, and both the Congress and past presidents, are culpable in expanding the complexity of the code.

These layers of carve-outs and changes have made it enormously difficult to make sense of the tax code. The Treasury Department's guide book on tax regulations, issued to help users interpret the meaning of the code, comprises six full volumes and sums to nearly 12,000 pages.

The code is so complex that 60 percent of Americans use paid tax preparers to complete their forms correctly. Another 20 percent rely on tax preparation software, such as Turbo Tax, to complete their forms. Even the IRs Commissioner admitted in a recent interview that he relies on a tax professional to complete his returns, in part because of the code's complexity.[63]

The average tax preparation fee for a standard itemized 1040 Form and an accompanying state tax return is just over $230, while small businesses pay between $500 and $700 for help with their forms, according to the National society of Accountants.[64] The total cost of complying with the individual and corporate income tax (gathering the requisite information, preparing the forms, etc.) amounts to over $160 billion per year, or 14 percent of all income tax receipts collected. To provide context, the money value of this drain on the nation's productivity is roughly three times larger than the amount the country spends researching and developing life-saving new medicine - pharmaceutical R&D amounts to around $50 to 60 billion per year.[65]

---

[61] "Roundtable Discussion On Ideas For Reforming The U.S. Internal Revenue Code,' Joint Committee on Taxation, May 11, 2011.
http:iiwww.jct.govipublications.html?func=startdown&id=3788

[64] 2011 Annual Report to Congress, U.s. Internal Revenue service, Office of the National Taxpayer Advocate, December 31, 2011.
http:iiwww.irs.goviadvocateiarticleio,,id=252216,00.html

[63] "Newsmakers with Douglas Schulman', *C-SPAN*, January 8, 2010. http:iiwww.c-spanvideo.orgiprogrami291155-1

[64]*NSA 2011-2012 Income and Fees Survey of Accountants in Public Practice*, National society of Accountants, August 3, 2011.

[65]*Pharmaceutical Industry Profile 2011*, Pharmaceutical Manufacturers Association, April 2011. http:iiwww.phrma.orgisitesidefaultiflesi159iphrma profile 2011 fnal.pdf

In the realm of tax policy, Congress sometimes focuses its efforts on improving tax compliance and trying to narrow the "tax gap' (i.e., the difference between what Americans owe in taxes and what the government actually collects). But the tax gap is merely a symptom of a complex and broken tax code. The best way to improve tax compliance and ease administrative burdens on the system isn't to enhance the enforcement power of the IRs - it is to dramatically simplify the tax code.

The Unfair Tax Code
All of the deductions, loopholes and carve-outs in the tax code don't just add to the code's complexity - they add to its unfairness as well.

The sum of all the special credits, deductions and loopholes in the tax code (so-called "tax preferences') amounts to over $1 trillion per year. To put that figure in perspective, that is roughly the same amount that the U.S. government *collects* in individual income taxes each year. In other words, these tax preferences end up narrowing the tax base by roughly 50 percent.

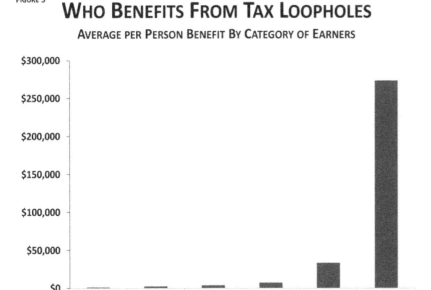

FIGURE 5

WHO BENEFITS FROM TAX LOOPHOLES
AVERAGE PER PERSON BENEFIT BY CATEGORY OF EARNERS

SOURCE: IRS/TAX POLICY CENTER

This is important for two reasons. First, because America has a highly progressive income tax, these tax preferences are disproportionately used by upper-income individuals (see Figure 5). For instance, the top 1 percent of taxpayers reap about 3 times as much benefit from special tax credits and deductions (excluding refundable credits) than middle-income earners and 13 times as much benefit than the lowest income quintile. And second, a narrow tax base requires much higher tax rates to raise a given amount of revenue.

A code with high rates and lots of loopholes benefits those who can afford the best lawyers and lobbyists in Washington. Instead of advocating for lower rates for all, those with political muscle usually take the path of least resistance by pushing for special deductions and carve-outs. This not only lowers their effective tax rates, but also enables them to use the complexities of the tax code to stack the deck against their competitors. There's nothing fair about that.

The Anti-Growth Tax Code

In addition to being complex and unfair, the code creates a drag on economic growth by being inefficient, uncompetitive and unpredictable.

Inefficient: The tendency of both parties to fill the tax code with loopholes also requires higher rates to compensate for lost revenue, resulting in a less efficient and less growth oriented tax system. Economic theory suggests, and most empirical studies prove, that marginal tax-rate hikes - tax increases that reduce incentives to work, save and invest for additional income above a certain cutoff - reduce economic output, while marginal rate reductions increase output, mainly by letting people keep more of each dollar they earn and thereby strengthening incentives to work, produce, and invest in the future.

FIGURE 6

TAX REVENUES DO NOT CORRELATE WELL WITH TAX RATES

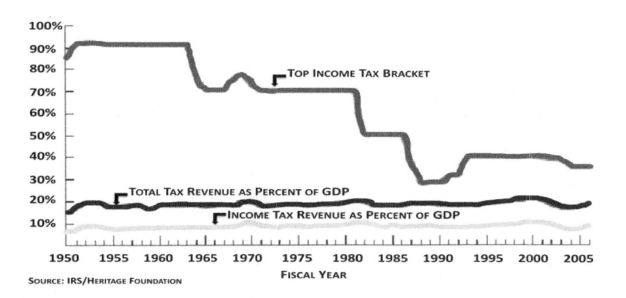

SOURCE: IRS/HERITAGE FOUNDATION

Lower economic output mutes the revenue effect of top-rate tax increases. Top rates have risen and fallen dramatically in the past, with little overall effect on tax revenue as a share of the economy. The top individual rate has ranged from 90 percent to 28 percent over the years, but income tax revenue has remained fairly steady despite these sharp rate swings.

The biggest driver of revenue to the federal government isn't higher rates - it's economic growth. Growth is the key to fiscal sustainability - and low rates are the key to growth.

Uncompetitive: The U.s. corporate income tax (incorporating federal, state and local taxes) sums to just over 39 percent, the second-highest rate in the industrialized world. Once Japan lowers its corporate rate, which it is expected to do on April 1, 2012, the United states will have the highest rate.[66] This tax discourages investment and job creation, distorts business activity, and puts American businesses at a competitive disadvantage against foreign competitors.

60

Cognizant of the stif competition in the 21st century global economy, many industrialized nations continue to *reduce* their corporate income tax rate.

FIGURE 7

TAX REVENUES ARE HIGHLY CORRELATED WITH GDP

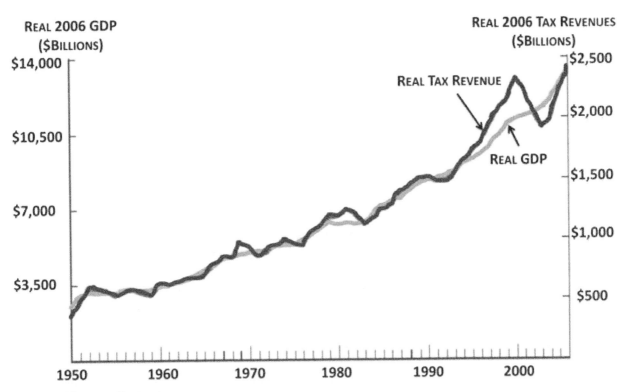

SOURCE: IRS/HERITAGE FOUNDATION

Yet the tax itself raises relatively little revenue - only 10 percent of total federal tax revenue comes from taxing corporate income. A 2005 CBO report reinforced this conclusion, stating that "distortions that the corporate income tax induces are large compared with the revenues that the tax generates.'[67] Any tax that creates such a significant amount of economic distortion relative to the revenue it raises is especially ripe for reform.

Like the individual income tax, the corporate tax contains a host of special carve-outs and deductions which serve to narrow the tax base by about 25 percent. This in turn necessitates the high rate that is undermining U.S. competitiveness.

[66] "Corporate Tax Reform Countdown,' House Ways and Means Committee,

http:iiwaysandmeans.house.govicorporatetaxreformi [67] "Corporate Income Tax Rates: International

Comparisons,' Congressional Budget Office, November 2005.
http:iiwww.cbo.goviftpdocsi69xxidoc6902i11-28-CorporateTax.pdf

Elevated corporate tax rates hinder American competitiveness by making the United States a less desirable destination for investment and jobs. Business location and investment decisions are becoming ever more sensitive to country tax rates as global integration increases. Foreign investment is important to an economy because it is a key source of innovation and jobs. In response, many countries have been lowering business taxes.

The United States risks falling behind as it maintains its high tax rate while other countries lower theirs. By deterring potential investment, the U.S. corporate tax restrains economic growth and job creation. The U.S. tax rate differential with other countries also fosters a variety of complicated multinational corporate behaviors intended to avoid the tax -such as profit shifting, corporate inversions, and transfer pricing - which have the effect of moving the tax base offshore, costing Americans jobs and decreasing corporate revenue.

The structure of U.S. international taxation is also out of sync with the standard used by the majority of other countries, and it puts U.S. businesses operating abroad at a competitive disadvantage. Most countries operate under a so-called "territorial' system of international taxation, whereby businesses earning income abroad are subject only to the tax system of the country where the income is earned. The U.s. has an antiquated "worldwide' system of international taxation, whereby U.s. multinationals pay foreign taxes on income earned abroad, and then U.s. taxes when the profits are repatriated. They are essentially taxed twice. This puts them at an obvious competitive disadvantage. Shifting to a territorial corporate tax system would boost the competitiveness of U.S. multinationals and reduce complex tax-evasion strategies, such as profit shifting and transfer pricing, that undermine job creation in the United States.

Empirical studies suggest that a reduction in the U.S. corporate tax rate could lead to significant economic benefits. One such study found that a 10 percentage-point reduction in the U.S. corporate tax rate could boost GDP growth per capita by 1.1 to 1.8 percentage points a year.[68]

Reforming the corporate tax system would have benefits for average U.S. workers and consumers, because they are the individuals who currently bear the costs of this flawed tax structure. Workers in particular could benefit from a reduction in the corporate tax rate. Another study from the CBO concluded that "domestic labor bears slightly more than 70 percent of the burden' of the corporate income tax.[69]

Corporations are not taxpayers - they are tax collectors, charged with collecting an unfair and inefficient tax from their shareholders, their customers and their workers. Investors pay the cost in diminished returns, consumers pay the cost in higher prices, and workers pay the cost in lower wages - or, worse, in the form of lost jobs.

Unpredictable: The expiration dates built into current tax law have left Americans exposed to a $4.5 trillion tax increase on January 1, 2013. This "tax cliff' includes the expiration of all current income tax rates, current tax rates on capital gains and dividends, the estate tax, the payroll tax holiday, the Alternative Minimum Tax, and numerous other tax provisions.

If all these provisions were to expire simultaneously, the impact on paychecks would be immediate, further eroding the take-home pay for families who are already struggling to make ends meet. The impact on markets would be disruptive: The prospect of a sudden snap-back in dividends and capital gains tax rates could precipitate a fight of capital away from job-creating businesses. And the impact on growth would be negative: If policymakers can't achieve this basic task of governance - ensuring low, predictable tax rates - then it is doubtful that job creators will have the certainty they need to expand, hire and grow the economy.

Both parties are to blame for this pile-up of expiring tax laws, for two reasons. First, Republicans and Democrats alike have in the past favored temporary tax changes over permanent ones, because temporary tax changes can be "scored' as having a smaller budgetary impact, even if it is well understood that these provisions are intended to be permanent.

[68] "Tax structure and Economic Growth,' *Journal of Public Economics*, June 2005 [69]William Randolph, "International Burdens of the Corporate Income Tax.' *Working Paper Series*, Congressional Budget Office, August 2006.
http:iiwww.cbo.goviftpdocsi75xxidoc7503i2006-09.pdf

Second, under the leadership of both parties, Congress has enacted temporary tax relief under the theory that short-term boosts in worker take-home pay would spur demand in a weak economy.

Neither of these reasons offers a good excuse for the uncertainty that this practice has forced American families and businesses to live with. The first substitutes budgetary gimmicks for responsible budgeting. And while there is nothing objectionable about letting people keep more of the money they earn, empirical studies have shown that temporary tax rebates - as opposed to permanent rate reductions - deliver very little "bang for the buck' in terms of economic stimulus.[70] Aware that their tax windfalls are temporary, most people do not make major changes in their spending habits. More importantly, temporary rebates do not strengthen incentives for increased work and productivity, which according to standard economic theory should be the aim of a pro-growth tax policy.

Nor do temporary rebates help businesses create jobs for American workers. Michael Wall - vice president of tax for Case New Holland, a tractor manufacturer which employs over 10,000 Americans - testified before the House Budget Committee last fall:

> "From our perspective as a business, we're looking for stable, permanent, pro-growth tax reform. Temporary incentives are temporary, as the name implies. When we look to make capital investments, we look at that return on investment based on a five-year cash-flow analysis. Right now, there's so much uncertainty with the tax code, there's not a permanent structure to really help us make intelligent decisions on where we expand our operations. So to answer your question, temporary is not helpful for us.'[71]

A Spending-Driven Challenge

Finally, it is worth noting that the U.S. government is not running sustained deficits because Americans are taxed too little, but rather because government spends too much.

Over the past 40 years, government revenue has averaged between 18 percent and 19 percent of GDP. This *level* has generally been compatible with prosperity, even though there is broad agreement that the *structure* of the tax code should be simplified and made more conducive to economic growth, high wages and entrepreneurship. Figure 8 shows that Washington has a spending problem, not a revenue problem. The President's budget would drive both spending *and* revenues to historic highs as a share of the total economy. The trend is clear: Chasing ever-higher spending with ever-higher tax rates would leave the economy at a severe disadvantage compared to the rest of the world, to say nothing of the pain felt by American families deprived of the chance to save for a better future.

[70] Matthew Shapiro and Joel slemrod, "Did the 2008 Tax Rebates stimulate spending?' *National Bureau of Economic Research Working Paper 13*, February 2009.
http:iiwww.nber.orgipapersiw14753

[71] Michael Wall, remarks before the House Budget Committee, *The Need for Pro-Growth Tax Reform*, September 14, 2011.

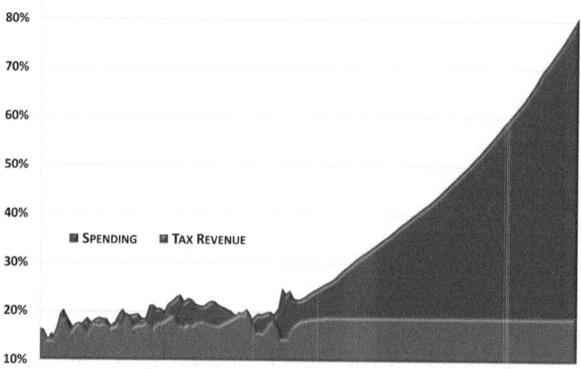

FIGURE 8 **WE ARE IN A SPENDING-DRIVEN DEBT CRISIS**
(AS A SHARE OF ECONOMY)

SOURCE: OMB/CBO

Nor can the government solve this problem just by raising the top individual tax rates: Even if it were wise to raise taxes on the most successful small businesses in America - most of which are owned by individuals and file at individual rates - the government cannot even come close to closing the fiscal gap that way.

The non-partisan CBO has concluded that the tax rates needed to sustain the nation's current fiscal trajectory into the future would end up sinking the economy.[72] That is one reason that the President's Fiscal Commission proposed, as part of an overall effort to fix the nation's unsustainable deficits, a fundamental tax reform plan that actually *lowered* income tax rates to promote growth, while eliminating tax loopholes to broaden the tax base.[73]

The Choice: Greater Complexity and Higher Rates vs. Pro-Growth Reform

To promote job creation and avoid major harm to the U.S. economy, policymakers need to replace the current mix of temporary rates and provisions with permanent, pro-growth tax reform. Unfortunately, the President and his party's leaders have called for the opposite approach - one that would hurt economic growth and endanger the weak recovery.

Greater Complexity and Higher Rates

The President has put forward a budget that calls for $1.9 trillion in higher taxes on American businesses and families. That's bad enough. But what's worse is that this new revenue comes, not from fundamental tax reform that lowers the rates and broadens the base, but from *higher* rates and added complexity in the tax code.

The President's budget would increase the top two income tax brackets from 33 percent to 36 percent and from 35 percent to 39.6 percent, respectively, starting next year. It would also restore the phase-out of personal exemptions and itemized deductions (the so-called PEP and Pease provisions) for this income group and limit the value of deductions against income.

When combined with the 3.8 percent Medicare surtax included in the new health care law, the President's tax policies would raise the top marginal tax rate to 44.8 percent (see Table 2). A "millionaire's surtax' proposed by leaders of the President's party in the senate would raise Washington's take of each marginal dollar earned to nearly 50 percent.

The President's budget would also increase the tax rate on capital gains from 15 percent to 20 percent for households making more than $250,000 ($200,000 for individuals) and would tax dividends at ordinary income tax rates (as high as 39.6 percent) - raising taxes on investing at a time when new business investment is critical for sustaining the weak economic recovery.

TABLE 2	
INCOME	
Top StatutorRate2011	35.0%
Expiratioo2001/03 Lower Rates2013	36.6%
PEP/PEASE Provision Re--Instated, 2013	41.6%
Net 2.3 Medicare Tax on Wages/Salary	43.9%
0.9Non--Deductable Medicare Tax, 2013	44.8%
DIVIDENDS	
Top Statutory Rate2011	15.0%
Tax DividendaOrdinarIncomRate2013	39.6%
PEP/PEASE Provision Re--Instated, 2013	41.6%
New 3.8% Tax on Investment Income, 2013	45.4%
CAPITAL GAINS	
Top Statutory Rate2011	15.0%
Expiration of Lower 2003 Rate 2013	20.0%
New 3.8% Tax on Investment, 2013	23.8%

" Congressional Budget Office, Letter to Congressman Paul D. Ryan, May 2008.

" "The Moment of Truth,' The National Commission on Fiscal Responsibility and Reform, December 2010.
http:iiwww.fscalcommission.govisitesifscalcommission.goviflesidocumentsiTheMomentofTruth12 1 2010.pdf

Instead of offering a plan for tax simplification, the President's budget would actually make the code more complex by adding new credits and deductions, as well as complicated new tax increases such as the so-called Buffett Rule, which would create a new minimum tax rate for upper-income families. To accompany the added complexity, the President's budget provides an additional $950 million to the IRs, which has an annual operating budget of nearly $13 billion.[74]

The President's own Treasury secretary admitted that the tax provisions of his latest budget would add complexity to the code, because, "if you try to get more revenues out of the current tax system in a rational way, you're going to do things that are complicated, there's no doubt about it and that's why it'd be better to do it through tax reform."[75]

Despite acknowledging that tax reform offers a better approach than the President's budget, the administration failed for the fourth budget in a row to include a comprehensive tax reform proposal. Instead, it waited until several weeks after the release of its budget to put forward a partial framework on tax reform, and even then its framework was limited to the corporate side of the code.

The administration's openness to lower corporate tax rates, while promising, falls far short of what is needed for comprehensive reform. Limiting reform to the corporate code creates a fundamental imbalance in the tax system because, as mentioned above, most of America's small businesses file their taxes as individuals. Reform should not tilt the playing field even further against small business.

Also, instead of moving towards a territorial system of taxation, which would remove economic incentives that encourage employers to keep profits overseas, the President's framework for corporate tax reform would move even further in the wrong direction by imposing a "global minimum tax' on corporations headquartered in the United states. Rather than having the desired effect of raising taxes on multinationals, this misguided approach would simply encourage existing businesses to move their headquarters abroad and new businesses to incorporate elsewhere.

The President's vision of higher tax rates for small businesses and more complexity in the tax code would exacerbate the problems with the current code and lead to economic decline.

Pro-Growth Reform

Led by House Ways and Means Committee Chairman Dave Camp of Michigan, this budget advances a framework that calls for an American tax system that is simple, fair and efficient to promote innovation and sustained job creation in the private sector.[76]

The House Ways and Means Committee held more than a dozen hearings devoted to tax reform last year. Last October, Chairman Camp formally released an international tax reform discussion draft, with proposals designed to boost competitiveness and job creation in the united states.[77] This budget reflects the progress that has been made over the past year by the House Ways and Means Committee, and calls for continued leadership to advance tax reform in the year ahead.

[74] "Fiscal Year 2013 Budget of the U.s. Government,' Office of Management and Budget, February 2012. http:iiwww.whitehouse.govisitesidefaultiflesiombibudgetify2013iassetsibudget.pdf

[75] Timothy Geithner, Testimony before the U.S. House, Committee on the Budget, *The President's Fiscal Year 2013 Budget: Revenue and Economic Policy Proposals*, February 16, 2012.

[76] This framework was outlined in a letter signed by every Republican member of the House Ways and Means

Committee. The reforms in this budget are inspired by the hard work they have done to advance the principles of fundamental tax reform. This letter can be found online at http:iibudget.house.goviUploadedFilesiWM.tax.agenda.pdf

⁷⁷ "Comprehensive Tax Reform,' House Ways and Means Committee, October 26, 2011.
http:iiwaysandmeans.house.govitaxreformi

This budget starts with the proposition that first, Congress must do no harm. It assumes that Congress will not allow massive, across-the-board tax increases to hit the economy in 2013. This budget then attacks complexity, unfairness, and inefficiency in the tax code with a set of fundamental reforms designed to lower tax rates, broaden the tax base, and reform the U.s. international tax rules, while getting rid of distortions, loopholes and preferences that divert economic resources from their most efficient uses.

Following the unveiling of a principled approach to tax reform in last year's budget resolution, an overwhelming consensus has emerged that the country is in dire need of tax reform that lowers rates, broadens the tax base, and addresses global competitiveness. After three years, the administration also has begun to recognize the need for tax reform. The outline for corporate tax reform released by the administration in February, however, falls woefully short: the rates are too high; the tax base is too narrow to benefit special interests; and the international reforms are anti-competitive.

By contrast, the principles of reform outlined in this budget ensure a simpler, fairer tax code not just for large corporations but for small businesses and American families as well. Unlike the administration's plan, it improves the competitiveness of American workers and businesses in the global economy. America's trading partners have already reformed their tax systems to provide their companies with a competitive advantage. Competing in a 21ˢᵗ century global economy requires that America do the same.

The Solution: Simplifying the Tax Code and Promoting Job Creation and Economic Growth

- **Reject the President's call to raise taxes.**

- **Consolidate the current six individual income tax brackets into just two brackets of 10 and 25 percent.**

- **Reduce the corporate rate to 25 percent.**

- **Repeal the Alternative Minimum Tax.**

- **Broaden the tax base to maintain revenue growth at a level consistent with current tax policy and at a share of the economy consistent with historical norms of 18 to 19 percent in the following decades.**

- **Shift from a "worldwide" system of taxation to a "territorial" tax system that puts American companies and their workers on a level playing field with foreign competitors and ends the "lock-out effect" that discourages companies from bringing back foreign earnings to invest in the United States.**

In 1981, President Ronald Reagan inherited a stagnant economy and a tax code that featured 16 brackets, with a top rate of 70 percent. When he left office in 1989, the tax code had been simplified down to just three brackets, with a top rate of 28 percent. Reagan's major tax reforms, enacted with bipartisan support without raising taxes, proved to be a cornerstone of the unprecedented economic boom that occurred in the decade during his presidency and continued in the decade that followed.

Over time, additional brackets, credits, carve-outs and lobbyist loopholes have undone the simpler and fairer tax code ushered in by the 1986 tax reform. In the last ten years alone, there have been nearly 4,500 changes made to the tax code. The current version for individuals has six brackets, with a top rate of 35 percent (which is set to climb to over 40 percent after the end of 2012, when hidden rates are considered). Individuals react negatively toward the tax code partly because it is complex and attempts to steer them toward certain activities and away from others. In addition, there are always a few "surprises' that end up raising their tax bills. One such surprise - the Alternative Minimum Tax (AMT) - was initially designed to hit only the very highest-income taxpayers but now ensnares a growing number of middle-income households because of a flawed design.

This budget affirmatively rejects President Obama's efforts to raise tax rates on small businesses and investors and to add new loopholes to the tax code for favored interests. Economic theory and analysis show that increasing marginal tax rates - tax increases that reduce incentives to work, save and invest that next dollar of income -reduces economic output. By contrast, reductions in marginal tax rates increase output, mainly by letting people keep more of each dollar they earn and thereby strengthening incentives to work, produce, and invest in the future. The House plan both realizes the job-promoting benefits of lower rates and ensures these reductions are revenue neutral through base broadening.

Unlike President Obama's proposal, the House plan would not penalize the nearly three quarters of America's small businesses that file taxes as individuals by imposing higher individual rates that make it harder for these vital enterprises to compete. As President Obama repeatedly says, small businesses have been responsible for two-thirds of the jobs created in the United States over the past 15 years, yet he often neglects to point out that roughly 50 percent of small-business profits are taxed at the top two individual tax rates.[78] Raising these rates means increasing taxes on the most successful job creators.
Raising taxes on capital is another idea that purports to affect the wealthy but actually hurts all participants in the economy. Mainstream economics, not to mention common sense, teaches that raising taxes on any activity generally results in less of it. Economics and common sense also teach that the size of a nation's capital stock - the pool of saved money available for investment and job creation - has an effect on employment, productivity, and wages. Tax reform should promote savings and investment because more savings and more investment mean a larger stock of capital available for job creation. That means more jobs, more productivity, and higher wages for all American workers.

The negative effects of high tax rates on work, savings and investment are compounded when a large mix of exemptions, deductions and credits are added to the system. These tax preferences are similar to government spending - instead of markets directing economic resources to their most efficient uses, the government directs resources to politically favored uses, creating a drag on economic growth and job creation.

In the worst cases, these tax subsidies literally take the form of spending through the tax code, because they take taxes paid by hardworking Americans and issue government checks to individuals and corporations who do not owe any taxes at all. In fact, President Obama's corporate tax "reform' framework would expand this practice by transferring taxes paid by middle-income Americans to the pockets of politically favored industries.

The budget would eliminate tax subsidies, not for the purpose of increasing total tax revenues, but instead to lower rates. This reform would have a doubly positive impact on the economy - it would stop diverting economic resources to less productive uses, while making possible the lower tax rates that provide greater incentives for economic growth.

There is an emerging bipartisan consensus for tax reform that lowers tax rates, broadens the tax base, and promotes growth and job creation. President Reagan's tax reforms inaugurated an era of great prosperity. It is time to build upon his leadership and advance a fundamental reform of the broken tax code as a critical step in rebuilding the foundations for economic growth: spending restraint, reasonable and predictable regulations, sound money, and a simple tax code with low rates.

[a] Brian Headd, "An Analysis of small Business and Jobs,' U.S. small Business Administration, March 2010.

http:iiwww.sba.goviadvocacyi849i7642j "Table 1.4 All Returns: sources of Income, Adjustments, and Tax Items, by size of Adjusted Gross Income, Tax Year 2008.'
Internal Revenue service. http:iiwww.irs.govipubiirs-soiio8in14ar.xls

CHANGING WASHINGTON'S CULTURE OF SPENDING

KEY POINTS

The refusal by some in Washington to adhere to the federal budget process has allowed government to spend recklessly and throw tax dollars at problems on an ad hoc basis as the nation's fiscal hole grows deeper.

This budget builds on the reforms advanced by the House Budget Committee to make the budget process more effective, accountable and transparent.

This budget establishes a binding cap on total spending as a percentage of the economy, making certain the federal government remains limited so the economy can remain free.

This budget extends the timeframe of the federal budget process to capture long-term unfunded liabilities, making certain that government fully accounts for its promises.

This budget reforms the Credit Reform Act to incorporate fair-value accounting principles, giving taxpayers a more honest assessment of the true costs of government loan programs.

This budget requires CBO to provide an assessment of the macroeconomic impact of major legislation, helping to address Washington's bias towards ever-higher spending.

CHANGING WASHINGTON'S CULTURE OF SPENDING

The Challenge: The Abandonment of Responsible Budgeting

Despite the best intentions of budget reformers over the years, mechanisms for spending restraint have broken down over time, and the rules remain stacked in favor of politicians who want to spend more money.

- The federal budget process contains numerous structural flaws that bias the government toward ever-higher levels of spending.

- Large swaths of the budget are not held accountable on a regular basis, and federal budget rules, which are written by Congress, assume that taxpayer money belongs to Washington, not taxpayers.

- The processes by which the federal government spends money lack the transparency that is needed for taxpayers to hold Congress accountable.

Budget process reforms alone cannot solve our spending and debt problems, but coupled with actual spending restraint and structural reforms to entitlement programs, budget process reforms are an important, if not critical, part of the equation.

The Choice: Spending without Restraints vs. Spending Cuts and Controls

When it comes to fixing the broken budget process, the choice facing Americans could not be more clear: The President and his party's leaders have failed to take their budgetary responsibilities seriously. By contrast, the Republican majority in the House met its legal and moral obligation by passing a bold budget that tackles America's most pressing fiscal challenges. More recently, the House Budget Committee authored and advanced several reforms aimed at bringing more accountability to the federal budget process.

Spending without Restraints

The President has delivered one unserious budget after another - none dealing with the nation's largest fiscal challenges. Three of the four budgets introduced during his term were late - shattering the record for any administration for missed budget deadlines.

While the President's budgets have been badly flawed, the U.s. senate has not passed a budget in over 1,000 days, and last year senate Democrats not only failed to pass a budget resolution: They failed to even *propose* one.

Spending Cuts and Controls

The purpose of budgeting is to offer the nation a vision for the country's future. Where there is a contrast between two visions, the budget process is intended to offer the American people an honest debate. But while the President and his party's leaders have shirked their duty to offer the nation that debate, the House has passed a bold budget that changed the conversation in Washington over the nation's fiscal crisis.

Not only have House Republicans met their obligation to budget, but they have also introduced and passed reforms to strengthen the budget process. These reforms adhere to the principle that the process needs to give policymakers new tools to bring spending under control; to get deficits and debt under control; to enhance oversight; and to increase transparency in the budget process.

The Solution: Changing Washington's Culture of Spending

Spending Control

- Replace the discretionary sequester in FY2013 with a new cap, and maintain enforceable discretionary caps on spending throughout the next decade.[79]

- Establish a binding cap on total spending as a percentage of the economy at levels projected to result from this budget resolution. Cap the total size of government, enforced by a sequester.

- Require any increase in mandatory spending to be accompanied by spending reductions (i.e., replace the current statutory "PAYGO" legislation with "CUTGO" legislation).

- Create a budget point of order against legislation that increases net mandatory spending beyond the ten-year window, a limitation that can help check congressional appetite to create costly open-ended entitlement programs.

- Close the loophole that allows discretionary limits to be circumvented through advance appropriations.

- Take mandatory spending of autopilot by capping major categories of this spending at the levels set forth in this budget, and reform the budget process to require a regular Congressional review of mandatory spending programs.

The spending Control Act (sCA), introduced last year by Representative John Campbell, would address the problem of out-of-control spending by establishing binding limitations on federal spending and deficits to provide Congress with a set of comprehensive controls as it addresses the nation's deficits and debt crisis. These limitations are in the form of statutory caps on the various categories of government spending and on deficits.

Enhanced Oversight

- Reform the budget "baseline" to remove automatic inflation increases in discretionary accounts and require a comparison to the previous year's spending levels.

Earlier this year, the House passed legislation introduced by Representative Rob Woodall to address this problem. The Baseline Reform Act would reform the baseline against which legislation is scored by removing the assumption that discretionary spending will automatically increase by inflation in each year of the baseline.

The legislation also requires the CBO to prepare an alternative projection of the baseline assuming the extension of current tax policies. Lastly, it codifes the current practice of the CBO providing a long-term budget outlook no later than July 1 of each year.

Full Transparency

- Extend the timeframe of the federal budget process to capture long-term unfunded liabilities.

- Require Congress to review long-term budget trends every five years and allows Congress to put federal spending on a sustainable path through a fast-track legislative process.

- Authorize reconciliation of long-term savings (beyond the current limit of the budget resolution's typical ten-year window) up to 75 years for Social Security, Medicare, and Medicaid. Require CBO long-term estimates beyond the ten-year window, and require the President's budget to extend beyond the ten-year window.

  The Balancing our Obligations for the Long Term (BOLT) Act, introduced last year by Representative Mick Mulvaney, builds on the statutory spending controls established in the Budget Control Act by extending those controls beyond the ten-year budget window. It also requires that Congress and the President consider the long-term fiscal impact of policy proposals.

  The BOLT Act also provides for enhanced information and analysis to be made available to assist Congress in the consideration of the long-term implications of the legislation. The CBO is required under the BOLT Act to prepare estimates of the long-term implications of major legislation in time for Congress to consider that information during its debates. Meanwhile, GAO and the Office of Management and Budget (OMB) would be required to provide annual analyses of the government's fiscal condition, specifically the long-term unfunded obligations of the U.S. government. The President's budget request would also be required to include long-term projections of the budget and of the policies proposed in that request.

- Reform the Credit Reform Act to incorporate fair-value accounting principles.

- Recognize the budgetary impact of the GSEs by formally bringing the entities on-budget.

  The Budget and Accounting Transparency Act, sponsored by Representative Scott Garrett and passed by the House earlier this year, increases transparency in federal budgeting by reforming the way certain costs are calculated and requiring that certain costs incurred by the federal government are included in the budget.

  Most importantly the legislation requires that in calculating the costs of federal credit programs (i.e., programs offering loans or loan guarantees), the executive branch and Congress use "fair value' methodologies that consider not only the borrowing costs of the federal government, but also the costs of the market risk the federal government is incurring by issuing a loan or loan guarantee or by making an investment in a private entity. This reform would bring federal budgeting in line with private-sector cost-estimating practices.

- Require CBO to provide an assessment of the macroeconomic impact of major legislation.

  The Pro-Growth Budgeting Act, sponsored by Representative Tom Price and passed by the House earlier this year, requires that, for major legislation, the CBO prepare an analysis of the effect that legislation could have on the U.S. economy. This analysis must include an estimate of the changes in economic output, employment, capital stock, interest rates, and tax revenues resulting from the enactment of the proposal. For purposes of this legislation, major legislation is defined as any legislation estimated by the CBO to have a budgetary effect of at least 0.25 percent of GDP (approximately $38 billion in 2011) in any year within the budget window. These analyses would cover the next 40 years.

LIFTING THE CRUSHING BURDEN OF DEBT

KEY POINTS

☑ This budget cuts government spending from its current elevated level of 24 percent of the economy to 20 percent by 2015.

☑ Relative to the President's budget, this budget cuts spending by more than $5 trillion over the next ten years.

☑ Relative to the President's budget, this budget shows more than $3 trillion in lower deficits over the next ten years.

☑ This budget sharply reduces publicly held debt as a share of GDP over its first ten years. By contrast, the President's budget drives the debt further in the wrong direction and allows government's fiscal position to "deteriorate" after that.

☑ The non-partisan CBO estimates that this budget will balance and begin to produce annual surpluses by 2040, and it will start paying down the national debt after that.

☑ This budget cuts debt by tens of trillions over time relative to the President's path to a debt-fueled economic crisis and permanent decline

LIFTING THE CRUSHING BURDEN OF DEBT

The Challenge: Debt-Fueled Economic Crisis Ahead

The United States faces a crushing burden of debt - a debt that just last year surpassed the size of the entire U.S. economy. If left on the course set forth by President Obama's most recent budget, the ever-rising debt will trigger an inevitable crisis and a state of decline that will be difficult, if not impossible, to reverse once it takes hold. In the years ahead, his budget concedes that the federal government's "fiscal position gradually deteriorates."[80] This admission is reminiscent of Ernest Hemingway's explanation of how one goes bankrupt: "Gradually, then suddenly."[81]

The United States has confronted extraordinary challenges in its past, both military and economic, from Pearl Harbor to the 9i11 terrorist attacks, the Great Depression to the Financial Crisis of 2008. In each of these cases, America's citizenry and her leaders were taken by surprise. But this time, the debt and the crisis that it will engender would be one of the most severe, yet predictable crises in the country's history.

The ongoing sovereign debt crises in Greece and other highly-indebted European countries provide a cautionary tale for America. Lenders cannot and will not finance unsustainable deficits forever, and when market forces provide a swift reality check for profligate governments, severe economic turmoil ensues.

In examining Washington's fiscal future, nearly every fiscal expert has warned that a major debt crisis is inevitable if the U.S. government remains on its current unsustainable path. The government's failure to prevent this completely preventable crisis would rank among history's most infamous episodes of political malpractice.

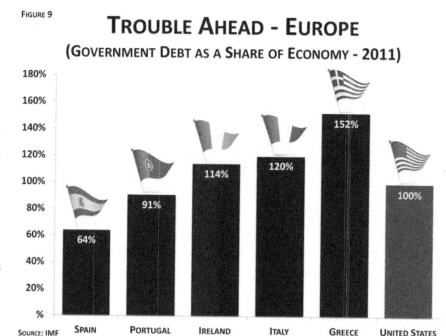

FIGURE 9

TROUBLE AHEAD - EUROPE
(GOVERNMENT DEBT AS A SHARE OF ECONOMY - 2011)

SOURCE: IMF — SPAIN 64%, PORTUGAL 91%, IRELAND 114%, ITALY 120%, GREECE 152%, UNITED STATES 100%

Debt as an Impediment to Growth

The debt is not just a far-of problem - it is having real effects today. In fact, the uncertainty associated with the government's unsustainable future is emerging as one of the primary factors currently weighing down the economy.

When the President took office in 2009, he and his party's leaders decided that the best way to boost economic activity would be to ramp up government spending dramatically through "stimulus' spending. But while this

76

spending provided a boon to politically connected industries and favored interest groups, it failed to deliver sustained economic growth and job creation.

[80] "Fiscal Year 2013 Budget of the U.S. Government: Analytical Perspectives,' Office of Management and Budget, February 2012.
http:iiwww.whitehouse.govisitesidefaultiflesiombibudgetify2013iassetsispec.pdf

[81] Ernest Hemingway, *The Sun Also Rises*. Scribner, 1926.

One of the main reasons this strategy failed is simple: It contributed to deficits soaring above $1 trillion a year, added trillions to the debt and increased the probability of a debt-fueled economic crisis hitting the United States. Americans know that today's large debt levels are simply tomorrow's tax hikes, interest rate increases, or inflation - and economic actors in the private sector respond accordingly.

In light of clear evidence that this stimulus spending did not achieve its promised results, there is a growing bipartisan consensus regarding the problem of growing debt and its detrimental economic impact. This debt overhang and the uncertainty it generates also weigh on U.S. growth, investment, and job creation today, because Americans make decisions on a forward-looking basis. Investors, businesses and families look at the size of the debt and the state of the economy and fear that America is heading for a diminished future.

Prominent economists argue that the key to jump-starting U.S. economic growth and job creation is tangible action to rein in the growth of government spending with the aim of getting debt under control. While all spending cuts need not take effect immediately, there is a growing urgency on setting forth reforms that curb Washington's spending appetite. The reforms themselves can - and should - be gradual, but locking in a fiscally sustainable path going forward can produce much needed certainty for economic actors *today*.

Last year, economists George Shultz, John Taylor, and Gary Becker wrote that, "Credible actions that reduce the rapid growth of federal spending and debt will raise economic growth and lower the unemployment rate. Higher private investment, not more government purchases, is the surest way to increase prosperity.'[82]

In addition to warnings from Shultz, Taylor and Becker, 150 prominent economists sent a letter to President Obama last year making clear that responsible spending restraint by the federal government would help foster a more conducive environment for job creation. In support of speaker John Boehner's proposal to ensure that any increase in the debt limit was matched by spending cuts of greater size, the economists - including two Nobel Prize winners - stated: "An increase in the nation's debt limit that is not accompanied by significant spending cuts and budget reforms would harm private-sector job growth and represent a tremendous setback in the effort to deal with our national debt.'[83]

Federal Reserve Chairman Ben Bernanke echoed a similar sentiment in a speech last year, saying that putting in place a credible plan to reduce future deficits "would not only enhance economic performance in the long run, but could also yield near-term benefits by leading to lower long-term interest rates and increased consumer and business confidence.'[84]

It is clear that if policymakers are serious about encouraging robust job creation, they need to chart a more sustainable fiscal course.

Nearing a Debt Crisis

In addition to being an impediment to growth today, the prospect of rising debt threatens American families and businesses with even greater economic harm in the foreseeable future.

Like a household or business, a nation's indebtedness is best understood in terms of how much it owes relative to how much it makes. By that measure, debt held by the public - money that the U.S. government owes to others - has reached nearly 70 percent of the entire U.S. economy.

[x] Gary Becker, George Schultz, and John Taylor, "Time for a Budget Game-Changer', *Wall Street Journal*, April 4, 2011. http:iionline.wsj.comiarticleisB10001424052748704471904576231010618488684.html

[x] "A Debt Limit Increase Without significant spending Cuts and Budget Reforms Will Destroy American Jobs', June 1, 2011. http:iiwww.speaker.goviUploadedFilesiECONOMIsTs-sTATEMENT-ON-JOBs-AND-DEBT-LIMIT-HIKE.pdf

[x] Benjamin s. Bernanke, speech to the International Monetary Conference, Atlanta, Georgia. June 7, 2011. http:iifederalreserve.govinewseventsispeechibernanke20110607a.htm

If this were merely a temporary rise in the debt, it would not be so alarming. However, the spending spree of the last two years, combined with the coming retirement of nearly 80 million baby boomers, threatens to turn these recent deficit spikes into a permanent plunge into debt.

Debt held by the public in excess of 60 percent of the economy is not sustainable for an extended period of time. That is bad news for the United States. According to the CBO, the President's budget would keep the debt climbing as a share of the economy in the decade ahead, from nearly 68 percent last year to over 76 percent of the U.S. economy by 2022.

How a Debt Crisis Would Unfold

The first sign that a debt crisis has arrived is that bond investors lose confidence in a government's ability to pay its debts - and by that point, it is usually too late to avoid severe disruption and economic pain. Right now, the U.S. government is able to borrow at historically low rates, partly because of the Fed's interventions in the market, but also because the bonds of most foreign countries are looking even riskier. Neither of these conditions is going to last. Interest rates - and the burden of paying interest on the debt - have nowhere to go but up.

Interest payments are already consuming around 10 cents of every tax dollar. But as interest rates rise from their current historically low levels and debt continues to mount, interest payments are projected to consume over 15 percent of all tax revenue by 2022.

That means that nearly one in six tax dollars will be dedicated to making interest payments by the end of the decade -and that's according to optimistic projections about interest rates. If interest rates increase by a higher-than-expected amount in future - which appears to be more likely - then the nation's interest payments could cost trillions of dollars more.

It would be one thing if the U.S. government owed most of this money to domestic lenders. But the nation's reliance on foreign creditors has increased dramatically over the past few decades. Foreigners now own roughly half of all publicly held U.S. debt, a sharp increase from a generation ago when foreigners owned just 5 percent of U.S. debt. This makes the nation vulnerable to a sudden shift in foreign investor sentiment, particularly during a time of crisis.

If foreign investors begin to lose confidence in the U.S. government's ability to solve its most difficult fiscal challenges, then they will demand higher compensation to offset the perceived risk of holding U.S. debt - meaning sharply higher interest rates.

During the financial crisis, foreigners flocked to Treasury debt simply because other investments looked so unsafe by comparison, and this helped keep interest rates low. But these investment flows work both ways, as the heavily indebted nations of Europe have recently learned. If the Congress continues to put of difficult choices regarding the nation's long-term problems, foreign investors will reevaluate the creditworthiness of the United States and demand higher interest rates.

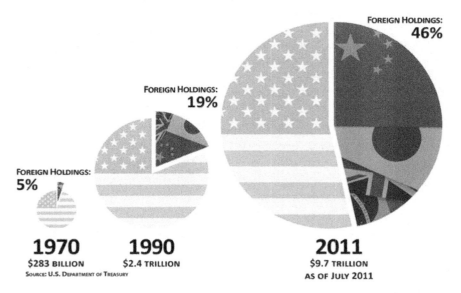

WHO OWNS OUR DEBT?
(DEBT HELD BY PUBLIC, 1970 -2011)

FOREIGN HOLDINGS:
46%

FOREIGN HOLDINGS:
19%

FOREIGN HOLDINGS:
5%

1970
$283 BILLION
SOURCE: U.S. DEPARTMENT OF TREASURY

1990
$2.4 TRILLION

2011
$9.7 TRILLION
AS OF JULY 2011

FIGURE 10

The Consequences of Inaction

The economic effects of a debt crisis on the United States would be far worse than what the nation experienced during the financial crisis of 2008. For starters, no entity on the planet is large enough to bail out the U.S. government. Absent a bailout, the only solutions to a debt crisis would be truly painful: massive tax increases, sudden and disruptive cuts to vital programs, runaway inflation, or all three. This would create a huge hole in the economy that would be exacerbated by panic.

Stagflation

Even if high debt did not cause a crisis, the nation would be in for a long and grinding period of economic decline. A well-known study completed by economists Ken Rogof and Carmen Reinhart confirms this common-sense conclusion. The study found conclusive empirical evidence that gross debt (meaning all debt that a government owes, including debt held in government trust funds) exceeding 90 percent of the economy has a significant negative effect on economic growth.[85] This is bad news for the United states, where gross debt exceeded 100 percent of GDP last year.

The study looked specifically at the United States, focusing on growth and inflation relative to past periods when this nation has experienced high debt levels. Not only is average economic growth dramatically lower when gross U.S. debt exceeds 90 percent of the economy, but also inflation becomes a problem.

Essentially, the study confirmed that massive debts of the kind the nation is on track to accumulate are associated with "stagflation' - a toxic mix of economic stagnation and rising inflation.

Real pain for families

Warning signs in financial markets would merely be a harbinger of the real economic pain that would eventually be felt by American families in the event of a debt crisis.

Much higher interest rates on government debt would translate into much higher interest rates on mortgages, credit cards and car loans. These higher rates would most likely come as a shock to most Americans, who have grown accustomed to borrowing in a climate of historically-low interest rates. It might even shock those who lived through the double-digit interest rates of the early 1980s.

Despite the increase in saving rates that has occurred in the wake of the financial crisis, U.S. households are still heavily indebted. The nation's households still owe $13 trillion in private debt, or roughly 120 percent of their total disposable income. A large chunk of that total debt consists of home mortgages, while the rest is in credit cards and other forms of debt.

It turns out that roughly half of all that debt is in the form of variable interest rate loans, meaning that a sudden increase in Treasury bond rates would lead to higher borrowing costs for consumers relatively quickly. According to the current level and composition of U.S. household debt, estimates suggest that an interest rate increase of just 1 percentage point would lead to over $400 in extra interest payments each year for the average family.

Given that a serious debt crisis could lead to a sharp increase in Treasury rates, the added interest costs for the typical family could easily exceed $1,000 per year. As household borrowing costs spiked, growth in overall consumer spending, which accounts for nearly 70 percent of the U.S. economy, would decline.

[85] Carmen M. Reinhart and Kenneth s. Rogof. "Growth in a Time of Debt,' American Economic Review Papers and Proceedings, January 2010.
http:iiwww.economics.harvard.eduiflesifacultyi51 Growth in Time Debt.pdf

Real pain for businesses

Higher borrowing costs would also serve as a serious impediment for businesses. The rise in interest rates would lead to lower business investment as companies would face a much higher hurdle for profitability on potential expansion plans. Businesses would be doubly squeezed because, as their funding costs were rising, demand for their products (particularly consumer durables bought on credit like cars, home furnishings, etc.) would be slipping as consumer spending tailed off. Add in higher taxes from a cash-strapped government trying to appease its creditors, and the inevitable result would be less business expansion and higher unemployment.

Harsh austerity

As economic growth deteriorates, it becomes harder for the government to raise revenue through taxes, and a vicious cycle ensues. If the nation ultimately experiences a panicked run on its debt, it will be forced to make immediate and painful fiscal adjustments (like the austerity program that has provoked riots and a deepening recession in Greece).

Facing the inability to borrow at a reasonable rate in the market, the government would have to slash spending and raise taxes to narrow its large fiscal gap. In such a crisis, the Fed may also face rising pressure to step in and "monetize' the government's debt - essentially printing money to buy up the public debt that private investors refuse to finance.

The consequences of these actions would be disastrous for the U.S. and the global economy. If the U.S. government were forced to address such a situation by cutting domestic spending and raising taxes to close the budget gap, it would be compelled to do so indiscriminately. Promises to current retirees would be broken, and tax rates would be raised across-the-board, without regard for the economic consequences. Monetizing the debt, meanwhile, would soon lead to a destabilizing inflation. This would wipe out the savings of millions of Americans, hitting seniors the hardest. When combined with benefit cuts, this would mean punishing seniors twice.

Financial system breakdown

The U.S. dollar is the world's reserve currency, and U.s. Treasury bonds are the lynchpin of global debt markets, considered to be safe and highly liquid assets by virtually all financial institutions worldwide. A U.S. debt crisis would lead to sharp declines in the dollar and in the price of these bonds, causing a deterioration of the balance sheets of large financial institutions. The resulting panic would be orders of magnitude more disruptive that than the financial crisis in 2008.

The Choice: A Path to Decline vs. A Path to Prosperity

Without bold new leadership, the unsustainable trajectory of the national debt will trigger a sharp and sudden debt crisis that would threaten national security, hit seniors and low-income Americans the hardest, and leave all Americans with a diminished future. This looming crisis represents an enormous challenge, but it also represents a defining choice: whether to continue down the path of debt, doubt and decline or put the nation back on the path to prosperity.

The President's budget offers a clear illustration of the former approach. By contrast, House Republicans offered a budget last year that would lift the debt and grow the economy. In response to the President's latest failure to lead, House has again offered another budget resolution that is equal to the nation's challenges.

A Path to Decline

After four budget submissions, the President has failed to use his term to confront the nation's most pressing fiscal and economic challenges. His fourth budget advances policies that dangerously accelerate the fiscal crisis America faces. His budget fails to reduce the fast-rising debt, entrenches unsustainable levels of government spending, and erects new barriers to upward mobility. His plan stifles economic growth, threatens the health and retirement security of millions of Americans, and commits the next generation to a diminished future.

Spending: President Obama's budget includes more of the same failed spending policies he has pursued since taking office - policies that would worsen the nation's fiscal crisis and speed the country to bankruptcy. Three years after the passage of the President's trillion-dollar spending stimulus, the President is at it again, calling for more wasteful spending taken from workers' paychecks or borrowed from abroad. The massive spending increases are greater than the few proposed spending reductions, for a net spending increase of $1.5 trillion over ten years.

Deficits: When he first took office, the President promised to cut the deficit in half by the end of his term. Four straight trillion-dollar deficits later, he hasn't even come close. His latest budget projects a deficit of $1.3 trillion for FY2012.

While some had hoped that the President might take some responsibility for breaking his promise, he has offered only excuses -for example, that the recession turned out to be deeper than he realized. But this excuse does not stand up to scrutiny: As recently as

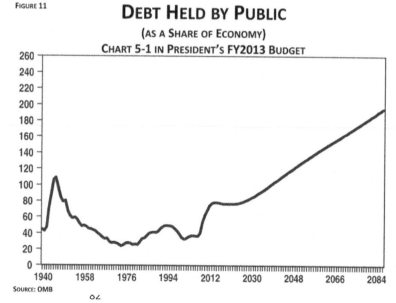

FIGURE 11

DEBT HELD BY PUBLIC
(AS A SHARE OF ECONOMY)
CHART 5-1 IN PRESIDENT'S FY2013 BUDGET

SOURCE: OMB

February of last year, well after the full extent of the recession was known, the President emphatically stated that he planned to keep his promise to cut the deficit in half, and provided projections to prove it.[86] This pattern - promising one thing, then delivering another - casts doubt on the President's latest round of promises and projections, which show deficits falling over time.

Debt: Under President Obama's watch, the federal government's total debt has surpassed the size of the economy - undermining job creation today and threatening a debt crisis tomorrow. According to its own numbers, the President's budget ignores the drivers of the debt, bringing America perilously close to a European-style crisis.

The President's own budget confirms that if policymakers continue down the present course, the consequences will be dire (see Figure 11 above). American families are still reeling from the hardships of the recent economic downturn, and millions of individuals remain out of work. Yet Washington continues to erect to new barriers to growth, to raise the hurdles to sustained private-sector job creation, and - most distressingly - to accelerate the nation ever-faster toward a debt-fueled economic crisis.

The CBO has warned that "persistent deficits and continually mounting debt would have several negative economic consequences for the United states. A growing level of federal debt would also increase the probability of a sudden fiscal crisis.'[87]

[86] Andrew stiles, "Obama's Deficit of Trust,' *Free Beacon.* February 15, 2012. http:iifreebeacon.comiobamas-deficit-of-trusti " "Federal Debt and the Risk of a Fiscal Crisis,' Congressional Budget Office, July 27, 2010. http:iiwww.cbo.goviftpdocsi116xxidoc11659io7-27 Debt FiscalCrisis Brief.pdf

Broken Promises: By failing to put forward long-overdue reforms, his budget allows social security to fall into bankruptcy (imposing an across-the-board 23 percent cut on seniors) and gives unaccountable government bureaucrats control over cutting Medicare in ways that would result in denied care for seniors. No credible action is taken to lift the crushing burden of debt. This President's empty promises are quickly becoming broken promises for millions of Americans.

A Path to Prosperity

This budget charts a brighter future. With responsible spending cuts now and structural reforms of government spending programs going forward, it ensures government spending remains on a sustainable path. This plan of action puts an end to empty promises from a bankrupt government, and instead restores the fundamental American promise: ensuring future generations inherit a stronger America, with greater opportunity than their parents were afforded. This unique American legacy - of leaving the next generation better of - must be restored. This is America's defining challenge.

The Solution: Lifting the Crushing Burden of Debt

Spending

Under this budget, government spending will fall from its current elevated level of 24 percent of the economy to below 20 percent by 2015. Restoring spending discipline in Washington is a necessary precondition for economic growth and job creation. While funding levels for government's core responsibilities and advance national priorities still grow, this budget ensures that government's role is limited and effective and that government spending is put on a sustainable path. As the economy grows, government spending as a share of the economy will steadily recede over the decades ahead. Relative to the President's budget, this budget cuts spending by more than $5 trillion over the next ten years.

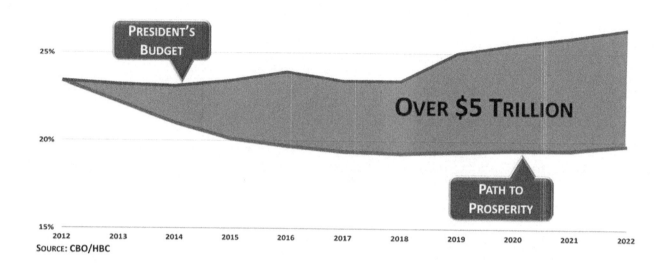

FIGURE 12

GOVERNMENT SPENDING

(AS A SHARE OF ECONOMY)

SOURCE: CBO/HBC

Deficits

This budget charts a sustainable path going forward, ultimately erasing the budget deficit completely. It brings the deficit below $800 billion in Fiscal Year 2013, whereas the President's budget would once again borrow close to $1 trillion. After four straight deficits in excess of $1 trillion - and a gusher of red ink over the next decade, the President's budget path never, ever reaches balance.

Relative to the President's budget, this budget shows more than $3 trillion in lower deficits over the next ten years. The deficit drops below 1 percent of GDP by 2016. And according to CBO estimates, it reaches balance in the years ahead, produces surpluses, and pays down the debt.

FIGURE 13

FEDERAL DEFICIT OR SURPLUS
(AS A SHARE OF ECONOMY)

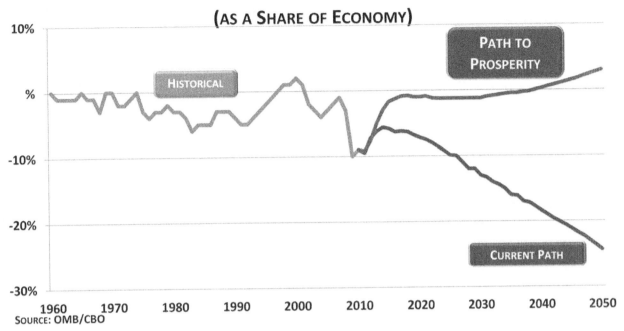

SOURCE: OMB/CBO

Debt

This budget tackles the drivers of our debt and averts the fiscal crisis ahead. This year, the nation's publicly held debt is projected to reach 73 percent of the economy - a dangerously high level that, according to leading economists, puts the nation at risk of a panicked run on its finances.

This budget tackles this crisis head-on by cutting debt as a share of the economy by roughly 15 percent over the next decade. The CBO estimates that this budget will produce annual surpluses by 2040 and begin paying down the national debt after that.

By contrast, the President's budget pushes debt as a share of the economy even higher. In his budget's own words, it allows the government's fiscal position to "gradually deteriorate' after 2022. This budget cuts debt by tens of trillions over time relative to the President's path to decline.

Keeping the American Promise
In the end, the debate about rising U.S. debt is not just about dollars and cents, but also about America's status as a world power and its freedom to act in its own best interests. If the nation stays on its current path, the United States will be unable to afford its role as an economic and military superpower. Other nations with very different interests will rush in to fill that role. Today's children will grow up in a world defined by different values, and their futures will be defined by fewer opportunities than their parents had.

Last year in *Foreign Affairs* magazine, financial historian Niall Ferguson surveyed some of the great empire declines throughout history and observed that "most imperial falls are associated with fiscal crises. All the cases were marked by sharp imbalances between revenues and expenditures, as well as difficulties with financing public debt. Alarm bells should be ringing loudly [for] the United states."[88]

America must not abandon its leadership role in the world. For this and many other reasons, Congress must act now to change the nation's fiscal course. The Republican House majority was sent here by the American people to get spending under control and confront these great challenges today to allow this generation to pass an even greater nation along to the next generation.

Congress can choose to let this nation go the way of fallen empires, or it can begin - today - the work of restoring the vitality and greatness of America.

[88] Niall Ferguson, "Complexity and Collapse: Empires on the Edge of Chaos.' Foreign Affairs, March April 2010.

House Budget Committee I March 20, 2012

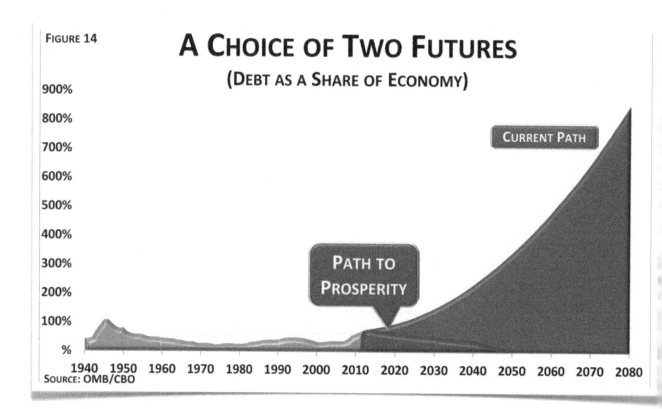

APPENDIX

Last year, as the nation approached the statutory limit on how much it could legally borrow, the Obama administration asked Congress for a "clean piece of legislation" to increase the government's legal borrowing authority without any spending cuts to match.[89]

House Republicans refused to give the President the blank check he requested. Instead, speaker of the House John Boehner insisted that any increase in the debt ceiling be accompanied by a greater amount of spending reduction. Speaker Boehner made clear on May 9, 2011 that, "Without significant spending cuts and reforms to reduce our debt, there will be no debt limit increase. And the cuts should be greater than the accompanying increase in debt authority the President is given."[90]

Once it became clear that Congress would not rubber-stamp his requested increase in the debt ceiling, President Obama announced that he would not accept a debt-ceiling deal that did not include large tax increases on American families and businesses.[91]

House Republicans succeeded in protecting hardworking taxpayers by preventing the President from securing a bill containing tax hikes. Instead, a bipartisan agreement was forged to achieve savings from limits on discretionary spending and to set in motion a framework to achieve additional savings. The Budget Control Act of 2011 (BCA) paired a $2.1 trillion increase in the public debt limit with equivalent deficit reduction over the ensuing ten years. The BCA called for deficit reduction in three phases:

1. First, it established caps on discretionary spending, achieving approximately $917 billion in savings over ten years.

2. Second, it established and called upon a Joint select Committee on Deficit Reduction (JsCDR) to produce legislation with at least an additional $1.2 trillion in deficit reduction.

3. Third, it established an automatic sequestration process to force spending reductions in the event the JsCDR did not produce a deficit-reduction bill or Congress refused to pass it. This "sequester' would result in immediate discretionary spending reductions effective January 2, 2013.

Understanding each component of the BCA is critical to understanding the fiscal impact of the law as a whole. The BCA's pre-sequester spending caps reduced discretionary spending for FY2013 to a maximum of $1.047 trillion. Some, including senate Majority Leader Harry Reid, are still insisting that House Republicans are obligated to pass FY2013 spending bills at these levels.[92]

But Congress is no longer operating in a pre-sequester world. Last November, the JsCDR announced that it could not reach agreement on a deficit-reduction bill by the statutorily required deadline, thus triggering the sequester. Congress is now operating in a post-sequester world - one in which discretionary spending for FY2013 is capped at $949 billion, and defense spending will be cut by $55 billion, or 10 percent, in January 2013 unless Congress acts to replace this sequester by reprioritizing the savings.

[89] Brian Patrick, "Debt Limit Tick Tock,' Blog Update, Office of Majority Leader Eric Cantor, August 1, 2011. http:iimajorityleader.goviblogi2011i08idebt-limit-tick-tock.html

[90] Remarks by House speaker John Boehner. Economic Club of New York. May 9, 2011. http:iiwww.speaker.goviNewsiDocumentsingle.aspx?DocumentID=240370

[91] Patrick, "Debt Limit Tick Tock.'

[92] Naftali Bendavid, "Fight Breaks Out Over 2013 Budget Cuts,' *Wall Street Journal*, March 14, 2012. http:iiblogs.wsj.comiwashwirei2012i03i14ifght-breaks-out-over-2013-budget-cutsi

These cuts would be devastating to America's defense capabilities. Leaders of both parties agree that sequester savings should be reprioritized. On August 4, 2011, then-director of the Office of Management and Budget (now White House Chief of staff) Jack Lew wrote that the sequester was not intended to be implemented: "Make no mistake: the sequester is not meant to be policy. Rather, it is meant to be an unpalatable option that all parties want to avoid.'[93]

The Joint Select Committee on Deficit Reduction

While both parties have expressed their desire to avoid the consequences of the sequester, there is profound disagreement over how. This disagreement was evident in the JsCDR's failure to produce a deficit-reduction bill last year.

Despite the good-faith effort on the part of committee Republicans to avoid the sequester (and, by extension, to avoid its disproportionate impact on defense), the negotiations exposed a fundamental lack of seriousness by some in Washington regarding the need to control government spending and address the structural drivers of the debt. As JsCDR Co-Chairman Jeb Hensarling made clear, Democrats on the committee "were unwilling to agree to anything less than $1 trillion in tax hikes - and unwilling to offer any structural reforms to put our health care entitlements on a permanently sustainable basis.'[94]

Committee Democrats refused to address the problem, so the problem remains. Therefore, the immediate question of how to reprioritize sequester savings - and the larger challenge of averting a debt-fueled economic crisis - have become central to this year's budget debate during this year's budget season.

[93] Jack Lew, "security spending in the Deficit Agreement,' August 4, 2011. http:iiwww.whitehouse.goviblogi2011i08i04isecurity-spending-defcit-agreement (accessed March 19, 2012).

[94] Hensarling, Jeb. "Why the super Committee Failed,' *Wall Street Journal*, November 22, 2011. http:iionline.wsj.comiarticleisB10001424052970204531404577052240098105190.html (accessed March 19, 2012).

The President's FY2013 Budget

The President's FY2013 budget calls on Congress to replace the sequester, but it does not make a specific proposal to turn the sequester of. It assumes that the sequester does not occur, but it does not lay out a specific path forward to avoid its consequences. The President's budget includes tax increases and spending cuts (including a $487 billion reduction in defense spending), which it claims are enough to offset the sequester - but it includes a net spending *increase* that consumes nearly all of its claimed deficit reduction.

This approach is deeply flawed, for three reasons. First, it imposes a net tax increase on American families and businesses of $1.9 trillion. Washington's fiscal imbalance is overwhelmingly driven by runaway spending, not insufficient tax revenue, and reducing the deficit by taking more from hardworking Americans would simply slow the economy, reduce job opportunities, and ultimately prove counterproductive as a deficit-reduction strategy.

Second, despite the large tax increase, the President's budget also contains a net spending increase of $1.5 trillion, for a total of only $400 billion in deficit reduction. The rest of the President's deficit-reduction claims are based on discredited budget gimmicks, including almost $1 trillion in "savings' that come from projecting current wartime spending in Iraq and Afghanistan out for the next ten years, then proposing not to spend that money, even though it was never requested and never going to be spent.

And third, much of the President's actual spending reduction comes from cutting too deeply into the Defense Department. Although the President's budget does not cut defense as deeply as the sequester would, these cuts would still jeopardize the capability of the U.S. military.

The Senate's Lack of a Budget

It has been three years since the senate passed a budget, and the legal deadline for passing a congressional budget resolution this year is fast approaching. Yet there has been no indication that senator Reid plans to put forward an alternative plan for prioritizing spending, much less for averting the sequester. Instead, he continues to insist that Congress is still operating in a pre-sequester world, even though the President's own budget admits that "the sequester was triggered and will take effect in January 2013 if no action is taken.'[95] senator Reid's approach has been the very definition of inaction. There is a better way forward.

The Path to Prosperity *Approach: Reprioritize Savings Through Reconciliation*

This budget reprioritizes sequester savings to focus on the problem, which is government spending, and to protect national security from deep and indiscriminate cuts. It achieves these goals by giving six House committees reconciliation instructions to produce actual legislation that achieves the sequester savings without the haphazard cuts that the sequester entails.

How Reconciliation Works

The 1974 Budget Act provides Congress with a special procedure to give expedited consideration to bills enacting the spending, revenue, and debt policies contained in the budget resolution. To trigger these expedited procedures, the budget resolution must include reconciliation instructions calling on specific committees to achieve specified amounts of savings in programs within their jurisdictions. The committees choose which programs to address and which policies to adopt.

Reconciliation in the FY2013 Budget Resolution

This budget gives reconciliation instructions to six committees - Agriculture, Energy and Commerce, Financial services, Judiciary, Oversight and Government Reform, and Ways and Means - that in aggregate would produce at least $18 billion of deficit reduction in the first year, $116 billion over the first five years, and $261 billion over the first ten years.

[95] "Fiscal Year 2013 Budget of the U.s. Government,' Office of Management and Budget, February 2012.

http:iiwww.whitehouse.govisitesidefaultiflesiombibudgetify2013iassetsibudget.pdf

House Budget Committee I March 20, 2012

Ultimately, the committees will be responsible for determining how to meet their reconciliation instructions. But savings could be achieved in the areas of making pensions for federal workers more like those for workers in the private sector, repealing recent expansions of the federal role in financial services, saving money in health care, means-testing entitlements, and reforming the medical liability system.

This budget provides a clear solution that would be implemented quickly to replace the sequester. It does so by using an expedited procedure to reduce lower-priority spending. This solution would cut through the gridlock in Washington to start eliminating excessive autopilot spending immediately. It would protect taxpayers, and it would shield the U.S. military from a crippling, 10 percent across-the-board reduction in its funding.

Unfortunately, the House cannot unilaterally implement this solution - and the senate Democratic leadership's only plan has been to oppose solutions put forward in the House. U.S. troops and their families should not have to suffer because the Democratic Party's leaders refuse to lead. House Republicans will continue to show a way forward by directly addressing the nation's most urgent fiscal and economic challenges. It is not too late for Americans to choose a better path.

Made in the USA
Las Vegas, NV
18 August 2021

28401972R00057